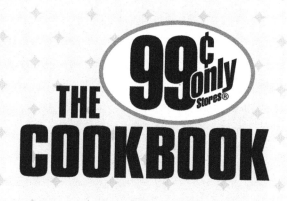

THE **99¢only Stores®**
COOKBOOK

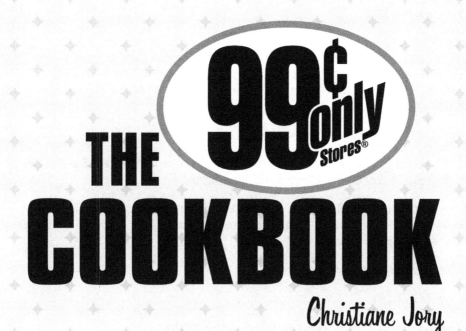

THE 99¢ only Stores® COOKBOOK

Christiane Jory

Gourmet Recipes at Discount Prices

Adams Media
New York London Toronto Sydney New Delhi

Adams Media
An Imprint of Simon & Schuster, Inc.
57 Littlefield Street
Avon, Massachusetts 02322

For information about special discounts for bulk purchases, please contact Simon & Schuster Special Sales at 1-866-506-1949 or business@simonandschuster.com.

The Simon & Schuster Speakers Bureau can bring authors to your live event. For more information or to book an event contact the Simon & Schuster Speakers Bureau at 1-866-248-3049 or visit our website at www.simonspeakers.com.

Manufactured in the United States of America

10 9 8 7 6 5 4 3 2 1

Library of Congress Cataloging-in-Publication Data
Jory, Christiane.
The 99 cent only stores cookbook / Christiane Jory.
p.   cm.
ISBN-13: 978-1-59869-469-7 (pbk.)
ISBN-10: 1-59869-469-3 (pbk.)
1. Low budget cookery. I. Title.
TX652.J675 2008
641.5'52—dc22
2007016522

ISBN 978-1-5986-9469-7

This book is dedicated to
Junie and Raymond
for cheering me along
every step of the way

Special thanks to
"Big Mike" at the
La Brea/Willoughby
location . . . and my
many fearless tasters

Contents

Hors d'Oeuvres and Appetizers ... 1

Sides and Soups ... 39

Main Courses ... 75

Baked Goods and Desserts ... 117

Foreword

by Sherry Gold and Dave Gold
FOUNDERS, 99¢ ONLY STORES

It was Friday the 13th in August 1982. An unusually long line of people wound around the small 2,500-square-foot store on La Tijera Boulevard in Los Angeles, which was about to open its doors for the first time. Excitement mounted as TV crews arrived, one after the other. The crowd of more than 500 people then surged forward. Each person felt that having waited in line all night entitled them to be among the first to enter the store, thus enabling them to purchase a brand-new TV set for 99¢ only. We started a tradition with those first nine people. Keeping up with the times, we have since sold iPods and other wonderful values to the first nine customers for 99¢.

We kept thinking that all the hype would die down, but the 99¢ Only Stores's customers kept coming—and come they have! Upper-income families, median-income families, even, reportedly, celebrities have come—ranging from Elizabeth Taylor and Richard Gere to Paris Hilton and Tyra Banks, who later filmed a TV show in the store. A world-renowned photographer, Andreas Gursky, took a photo in the store on Sunset Boulevard in Hollywood, which sold for more than $3.3 million on February 7, 2007, at the famous Sotheby's auction house in London—the highest price ever attained for a photograph. In addition, there is an annual event, a play, which demonstrates the great values consistently available at 99¢ Only Stores. All of the play's products, merchandise, and decorations come directly from 99¢ Only Stores.

Now there are more than 250 stores in four states. 99¢ Only Stores went public in 1996 and can be found listed on the New York Stock Exchange. Just as the first low-priced, high-quality products store grew and spread, so did the variety of items it carried. Products now include health and beauty aids, cosmetics, shampoos, vitamins, pharmaceuticals, house and garden products, tools, books, party aids and gifts, toys, back-to-school items, kitchen and bathroom cleaners, automotive products, and on and on.

But that's not what this book is about. Christiane Jory, a faithful customer of 99¢ Only Stores, has put together this great cookbook featuring ingredients purchased exclusively from 99¢ Only Stores. With each passing day, 99¢ Only Stores is selling a wider array of foods, including more fresh produce, dairy, fresh milk and eggs, fresh bakery products, deli items, and now organic items as well, so you can expand further on Christiane's recipes. She gives the steps for a wonderful dinner party for a large group, along with many helpful hints. Perhaps we will be invited. We'd be honored.

A Brief History

I moved back to Los Angeles eight years ago, and being introduced to 99¢ Only Stores has been my saving grace. I was quite skeptical when my friend Valerie told me about this futuristic dime store, and, like most 99¢ Only Stores neophytes, I pictured a dark warehouse full of dusty items, where only the most unwanted actually cost less than a dollar. So when I entered the La Brea and Willoughby location, I glowered and proceeded to search for the catch. Slowly my eyes widened and in a few moments I went from scoffing to gaping. "This is the best place on earth!" I exclaimed as Valerie reveled in the always-enjoyable "I told you so."

Even after this admission, I was still more of a sundry girl, not spending much time in the food aisles and retaining an appropriate amount of skeptical snobbery. Sure, every once in a while I would stop in before lunch and let my whining stomach talk me into buying some crackers or anything I could eat on the run, but as I explored the uncharted territory, certain items began to catch my attention—items like the same marinated artichoke hearts I had just spent $5 on at my local supermarket and, to my delightful surprise . . . the wine.

I never looked twice at the shelf boasting these vintages, until one day I noticed a woman, who would have looked more at home shopping in the Barney's shoe department, loading up her purple, metal cart with bottles of the 99¢ Chardonnay being offered at the time. I stared questioningly, and with a wink and a smile, she whispered, "It's really good." Well, now *I* am the woman (sans the fancy shoes) filling her cart with the newest 99¢ vintage and sharing the secret with chosen newcomers.

This personal history all came back to me a few years later when a group of friends and I were meeting at a French bistro in West Los Angeles. In the middle of a conversation my friend John trumpeted, "This is what it's all about . . . good friends, good conversation . . . some people, especially in this town, have it all mixed up. We are defined by *who* surrounds us, not *what* surrounds us. . . . This, my friends, what we have here is priceless." (I must point out that this happened before those credit card commercials coined the "priceless" catchword. John's quote, therefore, had more depth than it might today.) I agreed with him wholeheartedly, but refrained from ruining his epiphany by pointing out that this meeting of the minds was taking place in a forum that, though moderate, was not free, and that at least one of our friends was absent because of not being able to afford the "pricelessness."

It was a great night of laughter and debate and what I believe will be an addition to the fond memories of which life is composed. But am I going to remember the wine, the food, or even the restaurant when I am sitting in my rocker? Who knows, yet they were integral just the same. What I am sure to remember is that one of our friends was not there—and that is what kept nagging me after I arrived back home.

Armed with a glass of wine, I paced the length of my apartment while John's words played through my mind. Though reluctant, I was forced to admit that we were secretly under the control of what we had sworn didn't matter. Lack of funds had left one of us out that evening. But how could this have been avoided? We had long since moved beyond the point of hanging out in 7-Eleven parking lots, and playing host to six guests can run a small fortune—especially since "BYOB" is no longer in our vocabularies. I stared at the glass of wine, realized I had been taking my favorite store for granted, and had an epiphany. Never again would finances be a reason for not entertaining and cultivating memories of what, to paraphrase John's eloquent speech, life was all about. I would write a cookbook to prove it. The elements would come from my new food Xanadu. Besides being the cheapest, the variety was endless and the quality (as hush-hushed by my Chardonnay-packing friend years before) was there.

With that, I set the alarm clock and managed to doze off as my mind kept whirling over this new project.

I woke early and ran to my local 99¢ Only Stores, perusing the food aisles with a few rules. **ONE:** if an item was there even once, it was allowed to be included in the book. This wasn't too restricting, because one of the marvelous traits of 99¢ Only Stores is its reliability in keeping all sorts of products in stock. **TWO:** even if I had an ingredient at home, I still had to get it at the store, and had to use the actual brand and the form in which it was available so that every recipe would be truly tested. Take, for instance, sugar. Most of the time, the sugar available was sold in little coffee shop–style packets, a box of 100 for 99¢. So if you want to be fanatical like me, well, go ahead and open up eighty-two little packets for every cup of sugar you need. For you more reasonable folks, go ahead and use that bag of sugar you most likely already have at home. I struggled within these guidelines so that you wouldn't have to. After all, frugality starts with using what you've got.

Even though I was a child of the '70s and raised by a mother who embraced the new health-food era wholeheartedly, there were still culinary habits she couldn't quite shake. Being a child of the '50s, she was exposed to the instant-food sensations that saved her mother oodles of time in the kitchen. Cream of mushroom soup took the place of homemade stocks, rice cooked in a minute, and tuna casseroles could feed an army on a tight budget. So when parties were planned, the wheat germ got pushed to the back of the shelf, the fresh fruit desserts got replaced by slice-and-bake cookie dough, and the kitchen counters were loaded with opened cans of every kind of food imaginable. The first recipe in this book is a perfect example. Antipasto was my mother's fail-safe contribution to potluck cocktail parties, and since then the recipe remains the same with every ingredient being either bottled or canned.

Back at my 99¢ wonderland, the ingredients for the antipasto came together before my eyes. My first recipe! The inspiration was beginning to unfold and that was the day I opened my mother's trusty, avocado-green recipe box for the first time. In it I found not only the stepping-stones for this book, but a history that had been shelved since the time that box became mine. There were recipes on personalized stationery (a big trend in the '70s) from people I had not seen for years. There were notes on the backs of some of them that blew my mind, like "Pick Ginger up from vet" and "David's 6th b-day on Sat." So, as I was reminded of my very first dog and the cousin who introduced me to Led Zeppelin, I also found all kinds of recipes that would be perfect for my purposes.

Not only had I not set out to write a retro-style cookbook, but I certainly did not expect to re-experience my past in such detail. Not many people can pass 99¢ Only Stores without recognizing the Warholesque pop art displays of timeless items like Ajax and Arm & Hammer baking soda. So it began to make a sort of ironic sense that the answer to my modern day dilemma rested partly in that worn recipe box.

Food has its own meaning in every family, and having recipes passed down through generations can sometimes be as rewarding as looking through a photo album. I found that the further back in time I went with family recipes and my ancient cookbooks, the more clearly I remembered some of the financially "tight" times in my own childhood. Even then, there were always people eating, drinking, and laughing in our home. And keeping that alive was my whole mission in the first place.

I'll admit, in an ideal world we may all want to dine out regularly or have our own private chefs presenting us and our guests with cost-no-object delicacies at every meal. In this world, however, being able to serve hors d'oeuvres for twenty, dinner for eight, or brunch for twelve for about $29.99, to people we care about and without sacrificing taste—well, that seems pretty ideal to me.

Before you jump into the recipes, I highly recommend that you read the Equivalents and Substitutions section. I have included all the tidbits of information that I have gathered throughout my life and that I could not have written this book without. With this information, even gourmet recipes can be recreated in an affordable way. I encourage everyone to use this book not only for its recipes, but also for inspiration to create imaginative ones of your own.

Bon Appétit,

Christiane Jory

 **Menus**

Here are some sample menus to get you started.
Mix and match however you choose. Go wild!

Menus

Menus

Menus

Hors d'Oeuvres and Appetizers

.99¢
.99¢
.99¢
.99¢
.99¢
ABOUT
$12.99

Antipasto 20 SERVINGS

In the 1970s, this recipe was my mother's fail-safe cocktail party contribution. It took a little growing up for me to appreciate it. Call it "Tuna Tapenade" and it is immediately updated for the new millennium.

13 ounces Empress marinated artichoke hearts

2 (2-ounce) tins Polar flat anchovies

1 (12.5-ounce) jar Sunny Harvest cocktail onions, drained

2 (6-ounce) cans Smiling Sea tuna in water, drained

½ cup Di Buon Gusto olive oil

1 cup or ⅓ (26-ounce) jar Alfredo's tomato sauce

Tabasco sauce to taste

¼ teaspoon Chef's Choice garlic salt

½ teaspoon Spice Box Mexican chili powder

½ teaspoon El Pique oregano

½ teaspoon McCormick salt

½ teaspoon McCormick pepper

1 (15-ounce) can Veg-All mixed vegetables, rinsed and drained

4 ounces Forrelli mushrooms, pieces and stems

2 (4-ounce) jars Dromedary pimientos, chopped

¼ cup Sunny Harvest capers

½ cup Heinz sweet pickle relish

½ cup Heinz ketchup

¼ cup Prosperity white wine

¼ cup Luv Yu rice vinegar

1. Dice artichokes, anchovies, onions, and tuna.

2. Sauté oil and tomato sauce with spices and allow to cool.

3. Add vegetables to the sauce.

4. Add all remaining ingredients and refrigerate overnight.

5. Serve with crackers.

helpful hint

Inserting a straw to the bottom of a ketchup bottle will let in enough air to allow the ketchup to flow out nicely. This is less risky than pounding the bottle.

.99¢
.99¢
.99¢
.99¢
.99¢
ABOUT
$11.99*

Artichoke-Spinach Bake 12 SERVINGS

This recipe is great for parties. Trust me, no matter how much I make, it always disappears fast. It doubles, triples, and quadruples easily. For hors d'oeuvres, spread on a baked homemade pizza crust (see Pizza recipe in "Main Courses"), heat through, and cut into bite-size servings.

4 (6-ounce) jars Reese or Empress marinated artichoke hearts

2 (10-ounce) packages C&W frozen spinach, partly thawed, with the water squeezed out

Chef's Choice garlic salt

16 ounces Philadelphia regular or fat-free cream cheese

5 tablespoons Imperial margarine, plus some for the baking dish

¾ cup Springfresh milk

½ cup Aquila Parmesan/Romano cheese mixture

1. Grease a 9" x 13" baking dish with margarine.

2. Drain artichoke hearts and layer on bottom of dish.

3. Top with spinach and sprinkle with garlic salt.

4. Cream the cream cheese and add the margarine and milk, beating until well blended.

5. Pour over spinach and sprinkle with Parmesan/Romano cheese.

6. Cover and refrigerate for 24 hours.

7. Bake uncovered at 350°F for 40 minutes.

*$1.99 less if you use the 8-ounce packages of cream cheese. When I made this, only 1-ounce packages were available at four for . . . you guessed it, 99¢

helpful hint

In a jam, coconut milk can substitute for regular milk. Since coconut milk is canned, you can stock up.

.99¢
.99¢
.99¢
.99¢
.99¢
ABOUT .99¢
$1.99

Beet and Chive Toasts 4 SERVINGS

The rich color of the beets makes this an eye-catching appetizer. For hors d'oeuvres, serve a dollop of the beet mixture on Grilled Stars (see recipe at end of this section).

1 (15-ounce) can Libby's beets

¼ cup Spice Box dried chives

½ teaspoon Morehouse brown mustard

½ cup Knudsen sour cream

Tabasco sauce to taste

½ teaspoon Master's lemon juice

1. Coarsely chop beets.

2. Add the chives, mix in the remaining ingredients, and blend well.

3. Chill.

4. Serve on chilled plates with toast as an appetizer, or in a chilled bowl with a plate of toast for a buffet.

helpful hint

If you're game, a redhead, or both, reserve the liquid from the beets and use it as a hair rinse. Add three times the amount of water as there is beet juice and apply after shampooing for a temporary fun tint.

.99¢
.99¢
.99¢
.99¢
.99¢
ABOUT .99¢
$8.99

Gruyère Beignets ABOUT 36 HORS D'OEUVRES

These bite-size cheese fritters are easy to make just before company arrives. You won't be able to keep the plate full. They have been requested many times by my faithful tasters. Think mini calzones.*

Ideal vegetable oil for frying

1 package Golden Dipt beer batter or 1 cup Cinch pancake mix

1 can (less two swallows) Pabst Blue Ribbon beer

6 (4-ounce) packages Tiger Switzerland Gruyère cheese wedges, or approximately 36 ⅔-ounce pieces of your

preferred cheese, about the size of a rectangular tortilla chip ½ of an inch thick

1 (15-ounce) jar Alfredo's home-style tomato sauce with mushrooms (for dipping)

1. In a heavy-bottomed frying pan, pour enough vegetable oil so that wedges can float; heat to 375°F.

2. Prepare beer batter by mixing batter mix with beer (if using pancake mix, substitute the beer for the water called for in the instructions).

3. Stir until smooth. You may add more or less mix to get a thick enough consistency to batter the cheese.

4. Unwrap cheese wedges and dip into batter to evenly coat.

5. Fry coated wedges until golden brown, turning once for even cooking.

6. Drain on paper towels and serve hot with heated tomato sauce.

*Note: This recipe can be adjusted for different serving sizes. In this case, the amount was based on using all the Golden Dipt batter.

helpful hint

If you don't want to ingest the two swallows of beer, pour them into a shallow dish and place it in the garden near a plant susceptible to slugs or snails. Their taste for beer is stronger than their taste for your rhododendrons.

.99¢
.99¢
.99¢
.99¢
.99¢

ABOUT
$6.99

Chapatis 8 SERVINGS

Basic chapati is unleavened bread that is cooked on a griddle or right over a fire, which makes it puff up. Here it's the filling that's more true to the culture and using a pre-made dough shortens the preparation time.

1 cup Spice Box dried chopped onions (use fresh onions when available)

1 cup Premiere Fields lentils (use red lentils if available)

3 cups Harvest Choice frozen chopped spinach, thawed, with the water squeezed out.

2 tablespoons Danish Creamery butter

1 teaspoon Gilroy Farms minced garlic

½ teaspoon Spice Box curry powder

1 teaspoon McCormick salt

1 tablespoon Master's lemon juice

1 to 2 containers Pillsbury crescent roll dough (other dough will also work)

1 tablespoon Gold-N-Sweet vegetable oil

continued on facing page

helpful hint

Out of salt? Try soy sauce. It adds the missing element and an extra savory flavor as well.

Chapatis CONTINUED

1. Soak the dried onions in hot water for 5 to 10 minutes.

2. Drain and set aside.

3. Put lentils in a saucepan with enough water to cover and bring to a boil.

4. Cover and cook, until lentils are tender enough to be mashed with a wooden spoon, about 30–60 minutes depending on the age of the lentils. Add more water if necessary.

5. Stir in spinach and set mixture aside.

6. In a frying pan, melt butter and sauté onions until golden.

7. Add garlic and spinach/lentil mixture and fry, stirring until well blended.

8. Add curry powder, salt, and lemon juice.

9. Fry on low heat until liquid evaporates, stirring to ensure it does not stick to the pan.

10. Allow to cool and adjust seasoning to taste.

11. Prepare the dough on a floured surface by rolling into 8 balls and pressing them out to the size of a small saucer.

12. Put a spoonful of the lentil mixture in the center. Bring dough edges together and pinch to seal.

13. On the floured board, roll out the chapatis until they are as thin as possible without breaking and letting the filling out. They should once again be the size of a small saucer.

14. Heat a griddle very hot, spread the oil on it, and cook 1 or 2 chapatis at a time depending on griddle size. Press with a spatula while cooking, again being careful not to break seal. Cook until both sides are golden and speckled with brown spots.

15. Keep cooked chapatis covered with a cloth. When all are done, serve with remaining lentil mixture for an hors d'oeuvre or as an accompaniment to a main dish.

.99¢
.99¢
.99¢
.99¢
.99¢

ABOUT
$5.99*

Classic Fried Calamari with Tuna Caper Mayonnaise ABOUT 4 SERVINGS

Don't freak out when you open the cans of calamari! You may feel as if you are on Mars dealing with aliens, but as soon as you rinse and slice, you'll find yourself back safely in your kitchen.

2 cups bread crumbs made from
1 loaf Premium white bread or 2 cups
Manischewitz matzo meal

2 (15-ounce) cans Chicken of the Sea
whole calamari

2 or 3 Country eggs, beaten

Gold-N-Sweet vegetable oil for frying

1 cup Alfredo's tomato sauce with
mushrooms

Pique menudo spice mix to taste
(for tomato sauce)

1. To make bread crumbs, put oven on lowest setting possible.

2. Place slices of bread on oven rack and cook until they are dry and crumble easily in your hands.

3. Clean and cut calamari into bite-size rounds and tentacles.

4. Dredge pieces through eggs and coat with crumbs.

5. Fry until golden brown.

6. Drain and serve with warmed tomato sauce, or see recipes at right for other alternatives.

*With sauces

helpful hint

Egg whites can be frozen for future use without any special preparation. Yolks, however, should be beaten together with some salt—1 teaspoon for every 6 yolks.

8

Classic Fried Calamari with Tuna Caper Mayonnaise CONTINUED

TUNA CAPER MAYONNAISE

1 cup Albertson's mayonnaise

McCormick salt and pepper to taste

Splash of Citrovita white wine vinegar (red may be used)

2 tablespoons Sunny Harvest capers, rinsed

1 (6-ounce) can Chicken of the Sea tuna, drained and mashed

Combine all ingredients and refrigerate at least 1 hour before serving.

TARTAR SAUCE

⅓ cup Best Yet all-purpose flour or Cinch pancake mix

2 Country eggs, yolks only (these may be omitted if raw yolks are not desired)

1 cup Gold-N-Sweet vegetable oil

1 teaspoon Spice Supreme salt

2 tablespoons Citrovita white wine vinegar

2 tablespoons Master's lemon juice

1 teaspoon Morehouse brown mustard

1 cup Heinz sweet pickles, diced finely

1. Add enough water to flour to create a thick paste.

2. Beat egg yolks into the paste and blend well.

3. Gradually add oil, beating constantly.

4. Add remaining ingredients and chill at least 1 hour before serving.

ABOUT
$3.99

Corn Fritters ABOUT 20 HORS D'OEUVRES

These little delights remind me of succulent popcorn. Food Club diced green chiles mixed with Knudsen sour cream makes a great, creamy "chile verde" dipping sauce.

3 (15-ounce) cans Libby's whole-kernel corn

2 Country eggs

2 tablespoons Springfresh milk

1 large tablespoon Best Yet flour or Cinch pancake mix

¼ teaspoon Hearth Club-Clabber Girl baking powder

Pinch McCormick salt

Gold-N-Sweet vegetable oil for frying

1. Mix all ingredients together.

2. Form into quarter-size shapes and fry in oil until golden.

3. Drain on paper towels. Serve hot.

helpful hint

1 teaspoon of cream of tartar plus ½ teaspoon of baking soda can substitute for 2 teaspoons of baking powder.

.99¢
.99¢
.99¢
.99¢
.99¢

ABOUT
$0.99

Devilish Eggs ABOUT 10 HORS D'OEUVRES

The extra-hot sauces bring the devil back to what seemed to be a bland stint for these favorite snacks.

5 Country eggs

3 tablespoons Banquet mayonnaise

3 teaspoons Firey Louisiana hot sauce

1 teaspoon Tabasco sauce

1 teaspoon Spice Box curry powder

1 tablespoon Encore dried chives

1. Place eggs in a pot of cold water and bring to a boil.

2. Simmer 10 minutes more. Immediately drain and run under cold water. Peel when cool.

3. Cut eggs in half lengthwise and remove yolks.

4. In a bowl, mash yolks and add the remaining ingredients.

5. Blend well. Spoon this mixture into the egg whites, top with a dab of Tabasco sauce, and sprinkle with some dried chives.

6. Keep in the refrigerator until ready to serve.

helpful hint

A cracked egg will stay as fresh as the rest when the crack is sealed with a piece of Scotch tape.

.99¢
.99¢
.99¢
.99¢
.99¢
ABOUT
$1.99

Eggs à la Russe 6 SERVINGS

Since this is served chilled, it is a great summertime sit-down appetizer for anyone who likes deviled eggs.

1 teaspoon Spice Box dried chopped onions (use fresh onions when available)

6 hardboiled Foremost eggs

1 cup Albertson's mayonnaise

3 tablespoons Bali's Best chili sauce

1 teaspoon Spice Box dried chives

Dash of Tabasco sauce

Master's lemon juice to taste

1 teaspoon Chef's Choice parsley

1. Place 6 small serving plates in the refrigerator to chill while preparing the recipe.

2. Soak dried onions in hot water for 5 to 10 minutes. Drain and set aside.

3. Place eggs in a pot of cold water and bring to a boil.

4. Simmer 10 minutes more. Immediately drain and run under cold water. Peel when cool and halve lengthwise.

5. Combine remaining ingredients except for parsley.

6. On each of the cooled plates, place 2 egg halves, rounded sides facing up, and spoon the mayonnaise mixture over the eggs. Garnish with parsley flakes.

helpful hint

Hardboiled eggs turn rubbery when frozen. In the refrigerator they will keep nicely for 3 or 4 days.

.99¢
.99¢
.99¢
.99¢
.99¢
ABOUT
$5.99

Asian Chicken Tartlettes 30 SERVINGS

These are wonderful when guests will not all be arriving at once, since they are served cold or at room temperature. The filling can be made up to a day in advance. Assemble close to serving time to avoid sogginess.

1½ pounds Libby's canned chicken

2 tablespoons Pearl River Bridge soy sauce

1½ tablespoons Luv Yu rice vinegar

⅓ cup Gold-N-Sweet vegetable oil

McCormick salt to taste

McCormick pepper to taste

4 tablespoons Chef's Choice parsley

¼ cup Spice Box dried chives

30 shells made from 1 container Pillsbury buttermilk biscuit dough, or see Toasts, Cups, and Stars at end of this section for suggestions.

1. Preheat oven to 400°F.

2. Rinse and drain chicken. Set aside.

3. In a medium bowl, combine soy sauce, vinegar, and vegetable oil. Season with salt and pepper.

4. Combine sauce with chicken and add parsley and chives. Place in refrigerator while making the shells.

5. In a mini muffin tin, press a small amount of dough into each cup.

6. Bake for 3 to 5 minutes watching closely so as not to burn.

7. Remove from oven and let cool slightly. Fill prepared shells and serve.

helpful hint

The chicken in this recipe can be easily substituted with tuna for a nice variation.

.99¢
.99¢
.99¢
.99¢
ABOUT .99¢
$3.99

Clams Casino ABOUT 15 HORS D'OEUVRES

This is a classic that can also be made with oysters or mussels. In the original version, the filling would be put back into a half shell and quickly browned in a broiler. If you want the seared effect, place assembled hors d'oeuvres on a cookie sheet and broil for about 1 minute.

½ cup Spice Box dried chopped onions (use fresh onions when available)

8 tablespoons Danish Creamery butter

¼ teaspoon Spice Box paprika

Spice Supreme salt and pepper to taste

2 (6.5-ounce) cans Snow's chopped clams

12 slices Branding Iron bacon, cooked and diced

1. Soak dried onions in hot water for 5 to 10 minutes. Drain.

2. In a large frying pan, sauté butter, onions, paprika, salt, and pepper 2 minutes for the reconstituted onions or if using fresh, sauté until tender, but not brown.

3. Add clams and simmer for about 3 more minutes.

4. Serve warm, sprinkled with bacon bits on toasts of choice (see recipes at the end of this section).

helpful hint

Strain the bacon fat and use it to fry your next omelet. Store in the refrigerator for up to one week.

14

.99¢
.99¢
.99¢
.99¢
.99¢
ABOUT
$3.99

Golden Fried Oysters with Louisiana Mayo ABOUT 20 HORS D'OEUVRES

There is a Southern afternoon feel to these treats. They are great for a yard party and fun to prepare outside in an electric fryer. I have been known to fry them in a pan on the grill, but please use caution—hot oil on hot coals can be a dangerous combination.

3 (3.7-ounce) cans of Sunny Sea oysters

Cinch pancake mix or Best Yet flour for dredging

2 Country eggs, beaten

Martha White corn muffin mix for dredging

Gold-N-Sweet vegetable oil for frying

⅓ cup Louisiana Style hot sauce, more or less to taste

1 cup Banquet mayonnaise

1. Rinse and pat dry oysters. Dip oysters in pancake mix or flour, then into beaten egg, then into corn muffin mix.

2. In a heavy frying pan, heat oil until very hot but not smoking.

3. Carefully place oysters in oil and fry until golden brown.

4. Remove oysters from oil and drain on paper towels.

5. Mix hot sauce and mayonnaise and place in a ramekin on the center of a serving dish. Arrange oysters around ramekin. Serve hot.

*To remove the mayo, it's always best to work in the shampoo thoroughly before adding water. Otherwise the water may dilute the shampoo and leave some of the oily residue.

helpful hint

*A quarter cup of mayonnaise can act as hot oil treatment for dried-out hair. Apply to damp hair and scalp and blow dry for a few minutes; wrap hair in towel and relax for 15 minutes before shampooing out.**

.99¢
.99¢
.99¢
.99¢
.99¢
.99¢
ABOUT
$7.99

Jawa (Spicy Fried Meatballs) ABOUT 60 MEATBALLS

This is another dish that seems to exist in some form all over the world. There are Italian meatballs and Swedish meatballs; the Dutch call theirs *frikkadels* and the Spanish *albongidas*. The full name for the Javanese version is *pergedel goring jawa*. The spices in this recipe will be a nice surprise to the taster who assumes that the meatballs were prepared in the more bland European style.

1 cup Spice Box dried chopped onions (use fresh onions when available)

5 (14-ounce) cans Hereford meat balls in tomato sauce

2 teaspoons Gilroy Farms minced garlic

1 teaspoon McCormick salt

1 tablespoon Peppers diced fire-roasted jalapeño peppers or 2 teaspoons El Pique red chile flakes

1¾ cups prepared Idahoan instant mashed potatoes (you will need milk and butter/margarine)

1 tablespoon Pearl River Bridge soy sauce

1 tablespoon Master's lemon juice

2 teaspoons Spreckels sugar

3 teaspoons Encore Gourmet coriander

2 teaspoons Spice Box cumin powder

1 teaspoon Spice Box nutmeg

1 Country egg, beaten

Ideal vegetable oil for frying

continued on facing page

helpful hint

When sliced, diced, or chopped, a very cold onion is said to give off less-teary fumes than one at room temperature.

Jawa (Spicy Fried Meatballs) CONTINUED

1. Soak dried onions in hot water for 5 to 10 minutes. Drain and set aside.

2. Open meatballs and pour sauce in a separate container for another use. Rinse meatballs through a sieve and drain well.

3. Crumble the meatballs in a large bowl.

4. Add onions, garlic, salt, and chiles.

5. Add prepared mashed potatoes.

6. In a separate bowl, place soy sauce and lemon juice; dissolve sugar in the liquid.

7. Mix in coriander, cumin, and nutmeg.

8. Pour this mixture over meat/potato mixture and add beaten egg.

9. Mix thoroughly with hands and shape back into meatballs. Let stand for 1 hour.

10. Heat enough oil in a wok or frying pan to deep-fry. Fry up to 6 meatballs at a time. Since the meat used in this recipe is already cooked, fry for only 30 to 60 seconds, until heated through.

11. Arrange on a platter or in a large serving bowl with toothpicks on the side. Note: They can be served hot or cold, and are great for picnic snacks and sophisticated enough to be served as an hors d'oeuvre.

helpful hint

Like opening 82 packets of sugar (see introduction), rinsing and crumbling canned meatballs just to eventually reassemble homemade ones is based on what was available at the time.

It is very likely that you may find fresh ground beef on your shopping trip. Even better would be having some already in your icebox begging to be used before freezer burn ensues. The only adjustment would be to cook the meatballs longer (until golden brown around 5-8 minutes).

.99¢
.99¢
.99¢
.99¢
.99¢

ABOUT
$2.99

Nut-Stuffed Dates Wrapped in Bacon ABOUT 20 HORS D'OEUVRES

This classic recipe is a favorite and always a crowd-pleaser. I have also made these with ham slices when bacon is not available. They are tasty as well, but make sure you adjust cooking time since with ham they will only need to be warmed, not cooked.

1 (8-ounce) container Royal dates

1 (4-ounce) can Star Snacks mixed nuts

1 (16-ounce) package Branding Iron
hardwood smoked bacon

1. Stuff each date with any of the mixed nuts except peanuts (you can serve those in a bowl).

2. Slice bacon/ham into strips long enough to cover dates, preferably twice around.

3. Wrap each date with a piece of bacon/ham.

4. Secure with water-soaked toothpicks and bake on ungreased (or for easier cleanup, a foil-lined) cookie sheet for 5 to 10 minutes for ham, 12 to 15 minutes for bacon. Serve hot or at room temperature.

helpful hint

Instead of toothpicks, try using equally sized pieces of uncooked spaghetti. It will cook along with the dates and you will not be left to collect the unsightly used picks lying around.

.99¢
.99¢
.99¢
.99¢
.99¢
ABOUT
$1.99

One-Bite Ham and Cheese Pies ABOUT 12 HORS D'OEUVRES

These are spicy, cheesy bite-size biscuits. They can be prepared in advance, leaving out the last step of baking again for 1 to 2 minutes until right before guests arrive. My snobbiest, most skeptical friend loved them. Of course, I had to wait for her verdict before admitting they were part of the book.

½ container (about 8 ounces) Pillsbury buttermilk biscuit dough

1 (6-ounce) can Libby's chunks of ham

½ (5-ounce) jar Kraft Old English cheese spread

1 tablespoon Oscar Mayer real bacon bits

Eden Garden nacho sliced jalapeño peppers

1. Preheat oven to 400°F.

2. Peel the thinnest layers possible from the biscuit dough and form into the cups of a mini muffin tin.

3. Bake 3 to 5 minutes or until golden brown, watching closely to avoid burning.

4. Remove from oven and fill cups with a layer of ham, then cheese spread.

5. Sprinkle with some bacon bits and top each one with a jalapeño slice.

6. Bake again for 1–2 minutes, until cheese is bubbly. Serve warm.

helpful hint

These can be prepared and frozen in advance, allowing you to always be prepared for unexpected guests.

.99¢
.99¢
.99¢
.99¢
.99¢
.99¢

ABOUT
$2.99

Sardine Toasts à la Nicholas ABOUT 24 HORS D'OEUVRES

Given that my grandfather was Hungarian, I don't quite get how this very Italian recipe is attributed to him. I do know that it is the thin slice of butter that was his special touch.

1 (3.75-ounce) can Royal Fish sardines in oil

½ cup Master's lemon juice

2 Good and Fresh Arabic bread (pita rounds)

¼ cup Di Buon Gusto olive oil

McCormick salt to taste

McCormick pepper to taste

1 (4-ounce) jar Dromedary pimientos

6 tablespoons (24 thin slices) Danish Creamery butter

1. Preheat oven to 200°F.

2. Chop sardines and marinate in lemon juice.

3. Split each pita pocket into two flat rounds, for a total of four flat rounds. Cut into chip-size triangles, brush with oil, and season with salt and pepper. Bake until crisp.

4. Right before serving, use a cheese-slicer to make cuts of butter. On each pita chip, layer a thin slice of butter, some sardine mixture, and pimientos.

helpful hint

A little olive oil mixed into your cat's dinner will help prevent hairballs.

.99¢
.99¢
.99¢
.99¢
.99¢
.99¢

ABOUT
$1.99

Fried Spinach Balls ABOUT 10 HORS D'OEUVRES

Inserting toothpicks into these makes them guest-friendly, especially when served with a warm pot of garlic butter. Decadent? Yes, but too good to resist!

1 tablespoon Spice Box dried chopped onions (use fresh onions when available)

1½ cups Harvest Choice finely chopped frozen cooked spinach, thawed, with the water squeezed out

1 tablespoon Aquilla Parmesan cheese

Dash Spice Box nutmeg

1 Country egg, beaten with 4 tablespoons of water added

½ cup (about 11 crackers) Baker's Harvest cracker crumbs or ½ cup Martha White corn muffin mix

Gold-N-Sweet vegetable oil for frying

1 stick Danish Creamery butter (optional, for garlic butter)

1 teaspoon Gilroy Farms crushed garlic (optional, for garlic butter)

Spice Supreme salt to taste (optional, for garlic butter)

1. Soak dried onions in hot water for 5 to 10 minutes. Drain.

2. In a bowl, mix together spinach, onions, Parmesan cheese, and nutmeg and let stand 15 minutes.

3. Roll mixture into balls. Dip balls into beaten egg, then roll in crumbs or muffin mix.

4. Fry balls for 3 minutes in hot but not smoking oil.

5. Serve warm. If making the garlic butter, melt a stick in a saucepan, being careful not to brown. Remove from heat and add garlic and a dash of salt to taste. A raised ramekin with a tea light to keep the butter warm is recommended.

helpful hint

Coffee grounds rubbed on the hands or a coffee bean popped in the mouth is said to take the smell of garlic away.

Tea-Marbled Eggs with Spicy Peanut Sauce 12–24 PIECES

These eggs are little works of art. It is almost a shame to eat them, yet their beauty makes them so appetizing. Hardboiled eggs are a staple snack in many cultures. This Asian recipe has them lightly spiced as opposed to the European pickled version. They will make a beautiful addition to a selection of hors d'oeuvres.

6 Country eggs

4 cups of water

3 Covent Garden Ceylon tea bags

1 tablespoon McCormick salt

1 tablespoon Spice Supreme five spice seasoning

1. Place eggs in a saucepan and cover with cold water. Bring slowly to a boil, stirring gently to center the yolks within the egg. This will create a more uniform appearance once the egg is sliced.

2. Simmer gently for 7 minutes, then cool with running cold water for 5 minutes.

3. Crackle each shell by rolling on a hard surface. The more cracks, the more the egg will be marbled. Do not remove shells.

4. In a saucepan, bring 4 cups of water to a boil. Add tea, salt, and five-spice powder. Add crackled eggs. Simmer on low for 30 minutes, until shells turn brown.

5. Let eggs stand in covered pan for another 30 minutes or overnight.

6. Drain, cool, and remove shells. Halve or quarter the eggs depending on your presentation. Serve with a dipping sauce. I like these with the spicy peanut sauce recipe that follows.

Tea-Marbled Eggs with Spicy Peanut Sauce CONTINUED

SPICY PEANUT SAUCE

To mellow this sauce, eliminate the onion and chile flakes, and substitute ¾ teaspoon garlic salt for the minced garlic.

6 tablespoons Pica smooth or crunchy peanut butter

1 cup water

¾ teaspoon Classic minced garlic

1 tablespoon Spice Box dried chopped onions (use fresh onions when available)

El Pique red chile flakes to taste

2 teaspoons Spreckels sugar

2 tablespoons Pearl River Bridge soy sauce

Vanor coconut milk for thinning

Master's lemon juice to taste

Spice Supreme salt to taste

1. Soak dried onions in hot water for 5 to 10 minutes. Drain.

2. Put peanut butter and water in a saucepan, stirring over low heat until well blended.

3. Remove from heat and add garlic, onions, chili flakes, sugar, and soy sauce.

4. Add coconut milk as needed to turn this thick paste into a sauce with a pouring consistency. Then add salt and lemon juice to taste.

helpful hint

To distinguish between your raw and already cooked eggs, add a teaspoon of balsamic vinegar to the water when cooking the eggs. This will slightly tint the shell, making it easy to tell the difference.

.99¢
.99¢
.99¢
.99¢
.99¢
ABOUT .99¢
$9.99

Stuffed Yam Croquettes ABOUT 20 HORS D'OEUVRES

Delicious and quite filling! A warm snack for a holiday cocktail party.

½ cup Spice Box dried chopped onions (use fresh onions when available)

8 ounces Libby's canned ham

8 ounces Libby's canned chicken

¼ stick Danish Creamery butter

8 ounces Cheese Pleasers Asadero (jack) cheese

2 teaspoons Spice Supreme pepper, divided

3 (16-ounce) cans S&W candied yams, drained

1 tablespoon Encore garlic powder

1 teaspoon Spice Supreme salt

3 Country eggs

¼ cup Springfresh milk

1 cup Best Yet all-purpose flour

1½ cups Breakfast Choice corn flakes, made into crumbs

Gold-N-Sweet vegetable oil for frying

1. Soak dried onions in hot water for 10 minutes. Drain.

2. Sauté onions with ham and chicken in the butter over medium heat until nicely browned (if using fresh onions give them a head start since the meat is already cooked). Mix in cheese and season with 1 teaspoon pepper. Set aside.

3. Purée or mash yams until smooth. Mix in garlic powder, salt, and 1 teaspoon pepper until well incorporated.

4. Combine yams with the ham/chicken mixture. Divide mixture into 20 small bite-size balls.

5. Beat eggs and add milk to make a wash.

6. Dredge each ball through the flour, shaking of the excess. Dip into the egg wash and then roll through the corn flake crumbs.

7. Deep-fry for 7 minutes at 350°F, or pan-fry in oil over medium high heat, until golden and crispy. Serve hot.

helpful hint

When purchasing fresh yams, long and slender proves more sweet and tender.

.99¢
.99¢
.99¢
.99¢
.99¢
ABOUT
$5.99

Deviled Crab 6 SERVINGS

This can be served in one big dish with toasts on the side for a buffet, or individually in single-serving ramekins with a toast triangle placed in the center as a starter course.

4 tablespoons Danish Creamery butter

1 cup buttered bread crumbs or Manischewitz matzo meal

2 tablespoons Best Yet all-purpose flour or Cinch pancake mix

½ cup Springfresh milk

½ cup HyVee evaporated milk

¼ teaspoon Spice Box nutmeg

¼ teaspoon Morehouse brown mustard

2 Country eggs, yolks only, lightly beaten

¼ cup wine, white or red depending on preference (brands vary)

Spice Supreme salt and pepper to taste

3 cups Smiling Sea crabmeat, picked over, rinsed, and drained

Master's lemon juice, optional

1. Preheat oven to 400°F.

2. Melt 2 tablespoons of the butter in a pan, add bread crumbs or matzo meal, and stir until well blended. Set aside.

3. In a saucepan, melt 2 tablespoons butter, add the flour, and whisk until well blended.

4. In another saucepan, bring the milks to a boil. Add all at once to flour-butter mixture, stirring constantly until sauce is smooth. Remove from heat and add nutmeg and mustard.

5. Beat egg yolks with a little of the hot mixture, then add to the rest. Heat until thickened. Add wine, salt and pepper, and crabmeat.

6. Spoon mixture into 6 individual ramekins or one baking dish. Sprinkle with bread crumbs and bake until browned, about 10 minutes. Mist with lemon juice if desired.

helpful hint

⅓ cup of butter mixed with ¾ cup of milk can substitute for evaporated milk or cream.

.99¢
.99¢
.99¢
.99¢
.99¢
ABOUT
$3.99

Yummy Chicken Balls with Peanut Pesto ABOUT 16 PIECES

These are as delicious as any chicken satay. They're one of my fail-safe hors d'oeuvres for all of my non-veggie-loving friends. Gruyère Beignets would make a nice accompaniment to ensure there will be something for everyone. Serve with Peanut Pesto.

¼ cup bread crumbs, about 3 slices of Oliver's French country white bread, or ¼ cup Manischewitz matzo meal

3 (5-ounce) cans Crider white chicken

½ teaspoon Heinz Worcestershire sauce

½ teaspoon Master's lemon juice

1 teaspoon Encore dried parsley

1 teaspoon Encore dried chives

½ teaspoon Gilroy Farms minced garlic

1 Country egg

Gold-N-Sweet vegetable oil for cooking

1. Toast bread slices without crusts in a 200°F oven until dry but not browned. Crumble into crumbs and set aside.

2. Rinse and drain chicken well. Put in a bowl. With a fork, flake meat until very fine.

3. Add Worcestershire, lemon juice, parsley, chives, and garlic. Mix well

4. Add egg, then bread crumbs, and blend well.

5. Form into quarter-size balls and refrigerate for at least 1 hour.

6. Heat enough oil in a wok or frying pan and cook until golden brown on both sides. Serve hot with Peanut Pesto.

Yummy Chicken Balls
with Peanut Pesto CONTINUED

PEANUT PESTO 1½ CUPS

This is a must with the chicken balls, but can be used for anything with which a peanut sauce is desired. This recipe makes enough for twice the chicken ball recipe—since the balls will vanish quickly, you're better off doubling them.

1 cup Fisher dry-roasted peanuts

½ cup Pearl River Bridge soy sauce

¼ cup Teddy's syrup with honey

⅓ cup water

1½ teaspoons Gilroy Farms minced garlic

½ cup Pure sesame oil

½ teaspoon Spice Supreme black pepper

1. In a food processor, finely grind the peanuts.

2. With processor motor running, add the rest of the ingredients through the feed tube.

3. Mix until mixture becomes a smooth paste.

4. Refrigerate until ready to use. This will keep for up to three days.

helpful hint

When snipping fresh herbs from your garden, remember that 1 tablespoon of fresh equals ½ tablespoon of dried.

.99¢
.99¢
.99¢
.99¢
.99¢
ABOUT
$4.99

Mushroom Turnovers ABOUT 24 HORS D'OEUVRES

Mushrooms create some of the most familiar and best loved hors d'oeuvres. The woodsy undertone of the mushrooms combined with the spices and sour cream make for a mouthwatering experience.

FILLING

1 cup Spice Box dried chopped onions (use fresh onions when available)

3 tablespoons Danish Creamery butter

8 ounces Autumn Gold mushroom pieces

¼ teaspoon Spice Box sage

½ teaspoon Baja Pacific sea salt

McCormick pepper to taste

2 tablespoons Best Yet all-purpose flour or Manischewitz cake meal

¼ cup Knudsen sour cream

1. Soak dried onions in hot water for 5 to 10 minutes. Drain.
2. Heat butter in a frying pan. Add onions and brown lightly.
3. Add mushrooms and cook, stirring often, for about 3 minutes.
4. Add sage, salt, and pepper, and sprinkle with flour.
5. Stir in sour cream and cook on low flame until thickened. Set aside.

continued on facing page

helpful hint

1½ cups of fine bread crumbs can replace 1 cup of flour.

Mushroom Turnovers CONTINUED

DOUGH

9 ounces Philadelphia cream cheese, at room temperature

½ cup Danish Creamery butter, at room temperature

½ cups Best Yet all-purpose flour or Cinch pancake mix

1. In a bowl, mix cream cheese and butter thoroughly.

2. Add the flour and work with fingers until smooth.

3. Chill well, for at least 30 minutes.

4. Preheat oven to 450°F.

5. On a dusted surface, roll out dough to a one-eighth-inch thickness. Cut into rounds with a 3" biscuit cutter, or a jar with a 3" mouth.

6. Place about a teaspoon of the filling on one half of each round and fold the dough over. Press edges closed with tines of a fork and poke holes in tops to allow steam to escape.

7. Place on an ungreased cookie sheet and bake until browned, about 15 minutes. Serve warm.

.99¢
.99¢
.99¢
.99¢
.99¢
ABOUT
$5.99

Clam and Curry Butter Stars 24 HORS D'OEUVRES

Seafood and curry go very well together. Because curry has a big flavor, it is a perfect seasoning for these bite-size hors d'oeuvres.

½ cup Prosperity white wine

1 tablespoon Danish Creamery butter

1 tablespoon Baja Pacific sea salt

3 (6.5-ounce) cans Snow's chopped clams (can sizes vary; you will need the equivalent of 24 fresh clams)

24 pieces Oliver's white country bread

3 ounces curry butter (recipe follows)

¼ to ½ cup Spice Box dried chives

1. In a medium saucepan, mix wine, butter, and salt. Add ½ cup water, cover, and bring to a simmer. Add drained clams and cook for 2 minutes.

2. Remove clams with a slotted spoon, reserving all but ½ cup of the stock for another use. Pour the ½ cup of stock onto the clams to keep moist. Set aside to cool.

3. Heat oven to 300°F. Arrange bread slices on two baking sheets. Place sheets in oven; toast bread for 6 minutes each side. Cool on a rack.

4. Spread each bread slice with the curry butter and cut into stars with cutter.

5. Drain clams. Place on buttered stars, sprinkle with chives, and serve.

CURRY BUTTER

8 tablespoons Danish Creamery butter

1¼ teaspoons Spice Box curry powder

½ teaspoon Baja Pacific salt

Thoroughly combine butter, curry, and salt in a bowl. Roll in a cylinder and refrigerate until ready to use.

helpful hint

Leftover wine (as if there ever is any!) can go unwasted by freezing it in an ice cube tray. After cubes are frozen, store them in a freezer container and use them as a flavorful addition to savory sauces, soups, and gravies.

.99¢
.99¢
.99¢
.99¢
.99¢
ABOUT
$5.99

Baked Scallops ABOUT 40 HORS D'OEUVRES

Mussels can be substituted for the scallops if desired. This is a very economical and tasty choice for company.*

⅓ cup Spice Box dried chopped onions (use fresh onions when available)

3 slices Oliver's country white bread

2½ teaspoons Gilroy Farms crushed garlic

½ teaspoon Spice Box parsley

¾ cup Prosperity white wine

2 El Pique bay leaves

4 tablespoons Danish Creamery unsalted butter

1½ teaspoons Baja Pacific sea salt

½ cup water

5 (3-ounce) tins Polar smoked whole scallops

1. Soak dried onions in hot water for 5 to 10 minutes. Drain.

2. Preheat oven to 275°F.

3. Place bread, crusts removed, on rack and cook until bread feels dry to the touch but not browned. Leaving oven on, remove bread and let cool. Break into small crumbs and set aside.

4. Turn oven up to 450°F.

5. Combine onions, garlic, parsley, wine, bay leaves, butter, salt, and ½ cup water in a saucepan over medium heat. Bring to a simmer. Add scallops for 1 to 2 minutes, then transfer scallops to a separate bowl.

6. Turn heat up to high and cook until liquid reduces to one-half, about 6 minutes. Strain liquid and set aside.

7. Place scallops in a shallow baking dish and spoon reduced liquid on top. Sprinkle with bread crumbs. Cook until golden, about 5 minutes. Serve with toast of choice (see recipes at end of this section).

*Note: The scallops/mussels can be baked before topping with bread crumbs for 3 minutes, then placed individually on toasts sprinkled with bread crumbs and warmed for 2 more minutes. Or, depending on how much time you have for preparation, the dish can be set out with toasts on the side.

helpful hint

Pouring wine through a tea strainer will stop any cork bits from landing in the glass.

Spicy Corn and Pepper Spread ABOUT 2 CUPS

This spread is always an easy dish to whip up for unannounced guests. It can be made in advance, and the only maintenance required is keeping the bowl filled and the toasts of choice plentiful.

2 teaspoons El Pique whole cumin seeds, toasted

1 (15-ounce) can Libby's corn

1 (7-ounce) jar Dromedary pimientos

2 tablespoons Mi Mexico sliced jalapeños, chopped

⅓ cup Di Buon Gusto olive oil

Baja Pacific sea salt to taste

Spice Supreme pepper to taste

3 tablespoons Master's lemon juice

1. Preheat oven to 350°F.

2. Spread cumin seeds on an ungreased cookie sheet and toast in oven until aromatic, about 5 minutes.

3. In a mixing bowl, add corn, pimientos, jalapeños, and olive oil. Mix well, slightly mashing with a fork.

4. Add the remaining ingredients and chill for at least 30 minutes. Serve on toasts of choice (see recipes at end of this section).

helpful hint

A thin film of olive oil will give your face a moisturizing boost.

.99¢
.99¢
.99¢
.99¢
.99¢
ABOUT
$1.99

Crab Filling 1 CUP

This can be served as a spread or, as the name says, a filling. The flavor of the Corn Cups (see recipe at the end of this section) goes very well with this, as do the Ginger Jalapeño Rice Cakes on the next page.

4 ounces Philadelphia cream cheese

1 (6-ounce) can Chicken of the Sea crab meat, picked over and rinsed

1 tablespoon El Pique crushed red pepper, more or less to taste

2 tablespoons Master's lemon juice

McCormick salt and pepper to taste

Combine all ingredients and serve on toasts or cups of choice (see recipes at the end of this section).

helpful hint

When a recipe calls for the juice of 1 lemon, use ¼ cup of lemon juice.

.99¢
.99¢
.99¢
.99¢
.99¢
ABOUT
$0.99

Ginger Jalapeño Rice Cakes ABOUT 20 CAKES

These can be served with the Crab Filling or the Baked Scallops. If serving with the scallops, you can place the scallop dish on a bigger platter with the cakes surrounding it. It will make for nice presentation and is then self-explanatory. These can also be stored in an airtight container in the refrigerator for up to one day. Re-warm on a baking sheet at 400°F for about 5 minutes before serving.

1 cup water, salted

½ cup Robert's A-1 long-grain white rice

1 large Embassa jalapeño pepper, seeds and ribs removed, minced

1 Country egg

¼ teaspoon Spice Box ginger powder

¼ cup Best Yet flour, or 2½ tablespoons Manischewitz cake meal

½ teaspoon Hearth Club-Clabber Girl baking powder

1 teaspoon McCormick salt

3 tablespoons Di Buon Gusto olive oil

continued on facing page

helpful hint

To combat the heat after eating a chile pepper, try to eat milk, yogurt, or ice cream. Dairy products contain casein, which combats the effects of chile peppers' capsaicin by washing it from the skin. Sugar has also been said to help.

Ginger Jalapeño Rice Cakes CONTINUED

1. Bring 1 cup salted water to a boil.

2. Stir in rice. Reduce heat to simmer, and cover. Cook until water is absorbed, about 15 to 20 minutes. Transfer to a large bowl and allow to cool.

3. In a small bowl, combine jalapeño, egg, and ginger.

4. In another bowl, combine flour or cake meal, baking powder, and salt.

5. Add egg mixture to rice, then add flour mixture.

6. Spread mixture out on a 12" × 17" oiled baking sheet. Cover with an oil-brushed piece of wax paper or parchment paper, oil side down; press to even out.

7. Cover with plastic wrap and refrigerate for 1 to 24 hours, until firm.

8. Heat 1 tablespoon of the olive oil in a frying pan over medium high heat for 1 minute.

9. Slip spatula under rice and break up into two-inch squares—edges should be rough.

10. Slip cakes into frying pan and cook until golden, 3 minutes on each side. Drain on paper towels.

11. Continue to cook, adding ½ to 1 tablespoon of the oil for each batch of ten. Serve alone or with topping of choice.

helpful hint

Though its publication date is up for debate, an Ann Landers article is responsible for warding wedding goers from throwing rice. Apparently, the claim that it is fatal for unsuspecting birds is a myth. Her suggestion to throw rose petals instead is a lot nicer anyways. And why would anyone want throw perfectly good rice at their loved ones when it could be used to make these tasty treats?

Toasts, Cups, and Stars

Mix and match these with the fillings and spreads, as you like.

CORN CUPS

24 CUPS

$0.99

12 Guerrero corn tortillas

3 tablespoons Gold-N-Sweet vegetable oil

1. Preheat oven to 350°F.

2. Heat a large cast-iron frying pan.

3. Place a tortilla in the heated pan and cook for 20 seconds on the first side and about 15 seconds on the other. Remove from pan to a work surface.Brush both sides of the tortilla with oil. Using a 2½" round cutter, cut two rounds out of the tortilla.

4. Press a round into a cup in a 24-cup mini muffin tin. Repeat until tin is filled. Bake in oven until crisp and beginning to color, 5 to 10 minutes. Remove corn cups from tin and set on rack to cool.

GOLDEN CROUSTADES

24 CROUSTADES

$1.99

1 loaf Premium white bread, crusts removed to make 2½-inch squares

3 tablespoons Danish Creamery butter, melted

1. Preheat oven to 375°F.

2. Brush both sides of bread with butter.

3. Using your fingers, press each square into an opening of a 24-cup mini muffin tin. Bake until edges are golden, 5 to 8 minutes.

Toasts, Cups, and Stars CONTINUED

GRILLED STARS
ABOUT 30 SERVINGS

$0.99

1 loaf Premium white bread

1. With a star-shaped cookie cutter, cut two stars out of each piece of bread.

2. Heat a grill pan or outdoor grill over medium high heat.

3. Grill the stars until grill marks show, 3 to 5 minutes.

4. Cool on a wire rack.

5. Stars can be stored in an airtight container for 2 or 3 days.

HERBED PITA CHIPS
8 DOZEN CHIPS

$1.99

Add any spices you wish to the oil in ¼-teaspoon increments.

⅓ cup Di Buon Gusto olive oil

2 teaspoons Classic minced garlic

¼ teaspoon El Pique oregano, crushed (or spice of choice)

1 package (6 rounds) Good-N-Fresh Arabic (pita) bread

1. Preheat oven to 350°F.

2. Mix oil, garlic, and spices.

3. Split each pita pocket into two flat rounds, for a total of twelve flat rounds. Brush each round with oil mixture; cut into eight wedges and place on baking sheets.

4. Bake for 8 to 10 minutes or until crisp.

Sides and Soups

.99¢
.99¢
.99¢
.99¢
.99¢
ABOUT
$2.99

Asian Soul Slaw 8 SERVINGS

I personally never liked coleslaw until I was introduced to something that had more than just mayonnaise and cabbage as its ingredients. This recipe is a marriage of two of my favorites. It's got the complex tastes of the Asian ingredients with the kick of the Louisiana hot sauce.

1 (16-ounce) package Ready Pac coleslaw mix with carrots

1 cup Banquet mayonnaise

¼ cup Luv Yu rice wine vinegar

1 teaspoon Grey Poupon Dijon mustard

4 to 5 tablespoons Louisiana Select hot sauce

2 to 3 tablespoons Encore caraway seeds

2 tablespoons Pure sesame oil

2 tablespoons Ty Ling sesame seeds

1 teaspoon Spice Supreme salt

½ teaspoon Spice Supreme black pepper

1. Clean coleslaw mix and spin dry. Set aside.

2. In a mixing bowl, combine all other ingredients, blending well.

3. Pour over coleslaw mix and coat evenly.

4. Refrigerate at least two hours.

helpful hint

Nibbling on some caraway seeds is a tasty way to freshen one's breath.

.99¢
.99¢
.99¢
.99¢
.99¢

ABOUT
$3.99

Alu Bhaji (Savory Fried Potatoes) 4 SERVINGS

These are a great accompaniment to Naan (see "Baked Goods and Desserts") and also make a good filling for Chapatis (see "Hors d'Oeuvres and Appetizers"). When serving with the Naan, include a yogurt dipping sauce to balance this great snack. Since it is also delicious when cold it would be a nice variation of potato salad for a picnic.

1 cup Spice Box dried chopped onions (use fresh onions when available)

2 (15-ounce) cans Libby's whole white potatoes

1 tablespoon Albergo olive/canola blended oil

¼ teaspoon El Pique cumin seeds

½ teaspoon Spice Box turmeric

½ teaspoon Spice Box Mexican chili powder

1 teaspoon Baja Pacific salt

1. Soak dried onions in hot water for 5 to 10 minutes. Drain.

2. Rinse and drain potatoes. Boil in hot water to heat through without allowing the potatoes to get mushy. Remove from heat, drain, and dice.

3. Heat oil in a saucepan and fry cumin seeds until aromatic.

4. Add onions and fry until golden.

5. Add turmeric and chili powder. Stir, then add potatoes, sprinkle in salt, and toss to mix well. Serve hot or cold.

helpful hint

A slice of raw potato will keep down the pain and swelling of a bee sting.

.99¢
.99¢
.99¢
.99¢
.99¢
ABOUT
$4.99

Cabbage Skillet 6 SERVINGS

This is a good accompaniment to corned beef. It's a nice variation from the simple steamed cabbage that makes up the classic Irish dish.

2 tablespoons Spice Box dried chopped onions (use fresh onions when available)

4 (16-ounce) packages (8 cups) Ready Pac coleslaw mix with carrots

2 tablespoons bacon drippings, from Branding Iron bacon

1½ teaspoons McCormick salt

1 teaspoon Spice Box paprika

½ cup Knudsen sour cream

1. Soak dried onions in hot water for 5 to 10 minutes. Drain.

2. Cook cabbage and onions in bacon drippings in a 10" frying pan (preferably cast iron) for about 7 minutes or until tender. Stir frequently.

3. Add salt, paprika, and sour cream.

4. Heat thoroughly but do not boil. Serve warm.

helpful hint

The bacon needed to make the drippings for this recipe can be crumbled and stored in an airtight container in the refrigerator for up to five days for instant bacon bits on all your salads.

ABOUT
$2.99

.99¢
.99¢
.99¢
.99¢
.99¢

Corn Pudding 6 SERVINGS

Absolutely delicious! A cross between a bread and a soufflé. This is a great side dish all year long. I can't think of anything it won't go with.

6 tablespoons Best Yet all-purpose flour or 5 tablespoons Manischewitz cake meal

1 (15.25-ounce) can (2 cups) Libby's whole kernel corn

3 tablespoons Spreckels sugar

1 teaspoon Spice Supreme salt

4 tablespoons melted Dutch Farms Wisconsin Select margarine

1½ cups Springfresh milk

4 Country eggs

1. Preheat oven to 350°F.

2. Combine flour and corn. Add sugar, salt, and melted margarine.

3. In a separate bowl, beat milk and eggs together. Mix into the corn mixture and pour into a greased 9" × 13" baking dish.

4. Bake for 1 hour, stirring three times to ensure corn does not settle on the bottom. Serve warm.

helpful hint

Honey can be substituted for sugar, but remember it is twice as sweet. Start small and add more as you see fit.

.99¢
.99¢
.99¢
.99¢
.99¢

ABOUT
$4.99

Spicy Oyster Chowder 4 SERVINGS

This chowder is spicy and delicious. If you want to taper down the spice, add the menudo spice mix to taste. Serving this in a bread bowl ensures a pleased crowd and fewer dirty dishes!

1 (10½-ounce) can Baron condensed cream of mushroom soup

¼ cup Pique menudo spice mix

1¾ cup liquid from oysters, plus water to reach amount

1 (14-ounce) can Libby's creamed corn

2 (3.7-ounce) cans Sea Island smoked oysters, chopped

1 large or 4 individual round sourdough loaves (for bowls); Oliver's pretzel rolls are great if available.

1. Blend soup, spices, and liquid until smooth.

2. Add corn and cook 10 minutes.

3. Add oysters. Stir to combine.

4. Slice the tops off of 1 large or 4 individual rolls. Remove inside dough, fill with chowder and serve immediately.

helpful hint

An easy way to store soups is to pour the desired amount into a plastic bag, seal, and place in a plastic container with a height that exceeds the volume of the soup. Place container in the freezer; once frozen, remove the now stackable concoction.

.99¢
.99¢
.99¢
.99¢
.99¢
ABOUT
$6.99

Maine Corn Chowder 8 SERVINGS

Simple and wholesome. I kept this recipe in its original form because it brings back fond memories of cold days when I was young. But now that I'm older I like to add diced green chiles—or for a more dramatic presentation, green chiles mixed with sour cream and swirled into the soup before serving.

2 cups Spice Box dried chopped onions (use fresh onions when available)

8 slices Branding Iron bacon

3 cans (about 3 cups) Libby's whole white potatoes, diced

2 cups water

1 teaspoon Spice Box salt

Spice Box pepper to taste

2 (14-ounce) cans Libby's cream-style corn

2 cups Springfresh milk

1. Soak dried onions in hot water for 5 to 10 minutes. Drain.

2. Cook bacon in a Dutch oven until crisp. Remove and drain on paper towels, reserving drippings.

3. Sauté onions in drippings until golden, about 1 to 2 minutes.

4. Add potatoes, water, salt, and pepper.

5. Bring to a boil. Reduce heat; cover and simmer until potatoes are tender but not mushy.

6. Add corn and milk; heat through.

7. Garnish with crumbled bacon. Serve hot.

helpful hint

Wedges of raw potatoes can save an overly salty soup. To clean up the saltiness, add the wedges to the soup and let them soak up the extra salty flavor for at least 10 minutes. Remove before serving.

.99¢
.99¢
.99¢
.99¢
.99¢

ABOUT
$3.99

Green Beans au Gratin 4-6 SERVINGS

Even vegetable haters love this dish because it's so well disguised in its creamy, scrumptious sauce.

3 tablespoons Imperial margarine, melted

4 tablespoons Best Yet flour or Cinch pancake mix

½ teaspoon Spice Supreme salt

¼ teaspoon Spice Supreme pepper

1½ cups Springfresh milk

½ cup liquid from green beans

½ cup (about 6 slices) diced Whitehall Specialties American cheese

2½ cups Libby's canned French cut green beans

1. Preheat oven to 350°F.

2. In a saucepan over medium heat combine margarine, flour, and seasonings.

3. Add liquids gradually, stirring constantly.

4. Bring to a boil then cook 3 minutes more. Remove from heat and stir in cheese.

5. Place beans in a casserole. Pour sauce over and bake until top is bubbly and browned, approximately 30 minutes.

helpful hint

Be creative! Experimenting with different cheeses can keep this dish new and interesting every time you serve it. Pepper jack and goat cheeses are some of my favorite variations.

.99¢
.99¢
.99¢
.99¢
ABOUT .99¢
$2.99

Fried Pineapples 4 SERVINGS

Crispy on the outside, juicy on the inside—these are a great accompaniment to any ham dish.

1 (30-ounce) can Dole sliced pineapple, drained

1 (8-ounce) box Baker's Harvest crackers, ground to crumbs, or matzo meal

1 package Branding Iron bacon drippings, for frying

1. Coat each pineapple slice in cracker meal and fry until golden in bacon drippings.

2. Drain on paper towels and serve.

helpful hint

Cooking a roast with slices of pineapple can help tenderize an otherwise tough cut of meat.

ABOUT
$4.99

Hopping John 6 SERVINGS

This is like a not-so-soupy gumbo, and can definitely serve as a main dish. My tasters on the evening I served this, Kris and Carey, loved it! If you love things spicy like I do, you can add some sliced jalapeños to taste.

1 (16-ounce) can Allens Dorman black-eyed peas

3 (5-ounce) cans Libby's ham

½ cup Spice Box dried chopped onions (use fresh onions when available)

½ teaspoon McCormick salt

⅛ teaspoon El Pique crushed red pepper

2 cups water

1 cup Robert's A-1 uncooked rice

McCormick salt and pepper to taste

1. Soak dried onions in hot water for 5 to 10 minutes. Drain.

2. In a Dutch oven, combine peas, ham, onions, salt, and red pepper.

3. Cook 5 to 10 minutes over medium heat until heated through.

4. Add 2 cups of water and bring to a boil.

5. Stir in rice. Reduce heat; cover and simmer about 20 minutes or until rice is tender and liquid is absorbed.

6. Add salt and pepper to taste. Serve hot.

helpful hint

Uncooked rice placed in a salt shaker will soak up any moisture and keep that salt free-flowing.

ABOUT
$4.99

Texas Beans and Hominy 6 SERVINGS

Hominy is corn with the hull and germ removed. This process keeps the succulent corn flavor but makes the texture very smooth. If this turns you on, see the recipe for Hominy Cakes in "Baked Goods and Desserts." Mmmmm!

¾ cup Spice Box dried chopped onions (use fresh onions when available)

8 slices Branding Iron bacon, diced

1 pound Teasdale canned hominy, drained

1 (15-ounce) can Diamond A kidney beans, drained

8 ounces Alfredo's tomato sauce

2 tablespoons Food Club green chiles, chopped

1 tablespoon Citrovita red wine vinegar

1 teaspoon Morehouse mustard

1 teaspoon Heinz Worcestershire sauce

1. Preheat oven to 350°F.

2. Soak onions in hot water for 10 minutes. Drain and set aside.

3. Cook bacon in a frying pan until crisp. Remove and drain on paper towels. Reserve 1 tablespoon of the drippings in pan.

4. Sauté onions in the drippings for 1 minute.

5. Add hominy, kidney beans, tomato sauce, chiles, vinegar, mustard, and Worcestershire sauce.

6. Turn into a greased 1½-quart casserole dish. Sprinkle bacon over top. Cover and bake for 1 hour or until hot and bubbly.

helpful hint

It's always nice to give pretty bottles a new life: After washing, just squirt a little mustard into the bottle, fill with warm water, and shake it up. Rinse well, and any smell will be gone.

ABOUT
$4.99

Carrot Ring 8 SERVINGS

So retro and so good! This really will remind anyone old enough of those strange, round, colorful dishes that were so popular sometime between *Leave It to Beaver* and *The Brady Bunch*.

¾ cup Spice Box dried chopped onions (use fresh onions when available)

1 (15-ounce) can Libby's sliced carrots

1 cup Manischewitz matzo meal

1 cup Springfresh milk

¾ cup Kraft sharp cheddar cheese

½ cup Danish Creamery butter

¼ teaspoon Spice Supreme pepper

1 (15-ounce) can Libby's sweet green peas, rinsed and drained

3 Foremost eggs

1. Preheat oven to 350°F.

2. Soak dried onions in hot water for 5 to 10 minutes. Drain.

3. Boil carrots in a saucepan with their liquid and enough water to cover until tender. Remove from heat, drain, and mash. Set aside to cool.

4. In a bowl, combine all ingredients except peas and eggs.

5. Beat eggs until thick and foamy. Fold into carrot mixture.

6. Spoon combined mixture into a well-greased 1½-quart ring mold. Bake until firm, about 45 minutes. Serve ring with peas filling the center.

helpful hint

Washed, crushed eggshells around a house or garden plant can give it the much-needed calcium boost it's been begging for.

.99¢
.99¢
.99¢
.99¢
.99¢
ABOUT
$3.99

Maryland Crab Soup 4 SERVINGS

Red wine has been substituted for whiskey in this recipe. I have not strayed from the guidelines of this book, but you can. If you have some whiskey sitting around, go for it. It adds a nice nuance to the soup.

2 tablespoons Spice Box dried chopped onions (use fresh onions when available)

3 tablespoons Danish Creamery butter

2 (6-ounce) cans Chicken of the Sea crabmeat, rinsed and picked over

½ teaspoon Baja Pacific sea salt

McCormick pepper to taste

3 cups Springfresh milk

½ cup HyVee evaporated milk, or cream substitute

2 tablespoons red wine (use what is available)

Spice Box dried parsley

1. Soak dried onions in hot water for 5 minutes. Drain.

2. Melt butter in a frying pan. Sauté drained onions until transparent.

3. Stir in crabmeat, salt, and pepper and cook over low heat for 10 minutes, stirring occasionally.

4. Transfer to a double boiler or place saucepan over boiling water in a larger pot. Add milk and cook for 15 minutes.

5. Add the evaporated milk. When soup is piping hot, stir in red wine. Serve immediately, sprinkled with parsley.

helpful hint

Onions for Easter? Reuse onion skins by dying eggs. Wet onion skins, wrap around a raw egg, and secure with cheesecloth tied with a rubber band. Boil egg as usual; after you strip it, you'll find a purplish or golden naturally dyed egg.

.99¢
.99¢
.99¢
.99¢
.99¢
ABOUT
$5.99

Indian Chick Peas 6 SERVINGS

If you like Indian food, you'll love this. I particularly like it cold the next day. See the bonus recipe that follows for a version you can eat on the go.

1½ (15-ounce) cans (2 cups) Green Giant garbanzo beans

¼ cup Danish Creamery butter

1½ cups Spice Box dried chopped onions, reconstituted and drained (use fresh onions when available)

2 teaspoons Baja Pacific sea salt

1½ teaspoons Spice Box curry powder

½ teaspoon Spice Box ground ginger

½ teaspoon El Pique crushed red pepper

1 cup Sun Roma diced tomatoes

1 (14-ounce) can Sweet Sue chicken broth

1. Drain garbanzo beans, reserving their liquid.

2. In a frying pan, heat the butter. Add the onions and cook until lightly golden.

3. Add the seasonings and tomatoes and cook for about 10 minutes longer.

4. Combine tomato mixture and beans in a saucepan. Add the chicken broth and 1 cup of the reserved liquid to cover.

5. Cover and simmer for 20 minutes. Serve hot.

continued on facing page

helpful hint

A teaspoon of powdered ginger in a mug of hot water is a sure bet to help a tummy-ache. Don't forget the honey, Honey.

Indian Chick Peas CONTINUED

INDIAN CHICK PEAS ON THE GO

1½ (15-ounce) cans (2 cups) Green Giant garbanzo beans

1 tablespoon Albergo canola/olive oil blend

2 teaspoons Baja Pacific sea salt

½ teaspoon Spice Box curry powder

½ teaspoon Spice Box ground ginger

½ teaspoon El Pique crushed red pepper

1. Preheat oven to 400°F.

2. Drain and rinse garbanzo beans.

3. In a large bowl, combine oil and spices. Add beans and mix so that beans are well coated.

4. Spread mixture on a baking sheet. Bake for 30 minutes, stir, and bake for another 15 to 20 minutes, being careful not to let them burn. Cool and enjoy.

helpful hints

Chick peas, or garbanzo beans, are widely produced from India to Canada. They are a high fiber food source making them a great carbohydrate for those with insulin sensitivity.

.99¢
.99¢
.99¢
.99¢
.99¢
ABOUT
$4.99

Creamed Asparagus 4-6 SERVINGS

Another well-disguised vegetable dish. With the plethora of ingredients, even those "allergic" to vegetables will love this.

¼ cup Danish Creamery butter

¼ cup Best Yet all-purpose flour or 2½ tablespoons Manischewitz cake meal

1 (14.5-ounce) can (1¾ cups) Sweet Sue chicken broth

¼ cup HyVee evaporated milk

Pinch Spice Box nutmeg

Spice Supreme salt and pepper to taste

3 hardboiled Country eggs

1 cup Hormel canned ham

24 Pacific Friend asparagus spears

Aquilla Romano/Parmesan grated cheese

1. Preheat oven to 400°F.

2. Melt butter in a saucepan. Add the flour and whisk until blended.

3. Meanwhile, bring the broth and milk to a boil. Add all at once to butter-flour mixture, stirring constantly until sauce is thick and smooth. Season with nutmeg, salt, and pepper.

4. Butter a casserole dish. Place alternating layers of sauce, eggs, ham, and asparagus in dish, ending with sauce.

5. Sprinkle cheese on top and bake for 5 to 10 minutes.

helpful hint

Letting raw eggs stand in warm water before boiling helps prevent cracking.

.99¢
.99¢
.99¢
.99¢
ABOUT .99¢
$3.99

Gingered Beets 4 SERVINGS

A delightful sweet and tangy dish, aesthetically and tastefully pleasing.

⅓ cup Spreckels sugar

¾ teaspoon Spice Box ground ginger

2 teaspoons Hartford House cornstarch

¼ cup Citrovita apple cider vinegar

2½ cups Libby's canned beets, drained

2 tablespoons Danish Creamery butter

1 tablespoon Spice Box chopped parsley

1. In a saucepan, blend sugar, ginger, and cornstarch and gradually add the vinegar. Stir until smooth.

2. Cook over medium heat, stirring until thick.

3. Add the beets and butter and simmer for 10 minutes, stirring occasionally.

4. Serve hot sprinkled with parsley.

helpful hint

A teaspoon of apple cider vinegar a day helps keep the doctor away. I like it with sparkling water and a dash of bitters.

.99¢
.99¢
.99¢
.99¢
ABOUT
$1.99
or **$4.99**

Coconut Milk Rice 6 SERVINGS

This is perfect with any curry dish or any time you want to jazz up plain old white rice. There are two versions here. The first is milder, and when sprinkled with sugar can also serve as a lovely breakfast.

VERSION 1

2 cups Thai Lady jasmine rice

3 cups water

2 cups Vanor coconut milk

2 teaspoons McCormick salt

1 Spice Supreme cinnamon stick

1. Put rice and water into a saucepan and bring to a boil.

2. Cover and cook 15 minutes.

3. Add coconut milk, salt, and cinnamon stick, stirring with a wooden spoon. Cover and cook on very low heat for 10 to 15 minutes, until liquid is absorbed.

4. Remove cinnamon stick and serve warm or cool.

continued on facing page

helpful hint

If faced with a fresh coconut, do not fret. First, search out the black "eyes." Then, using a Phillips-head screwdriver and a hammer, make a hole in each one. Finally, one hit with the hammer on this same area should open the coconut right up.

Coconut Milk Rice CONTINUED

This second variation is strictly savory and has kick.

VERSION 2

1 pound Robert's A-1 white rice

4½ cups Vanor coconut milk

2½ teaspoon Baja Pacific salt

1 cup Spice Box dried chopped onions
(use fresh onions when available)

2 teaspoons Gilroy Farms minced garlic

1 teaspoon Spice Box turmeric

1 teaspoon El Pique ground cumin

2 teaspoons Encore Gourmet ground coriander

El Pique red chile flakes to taste

1 teaspoon Master's lemon juice

1. Wash and drain rice.

2. Put all ingredients except for the rice in a saucepan with a tight-fitting lid.

3. Bring to a slow boil, uncovered, stirring often. Add rice, bring back to a boil, then turn heat as low as possible.

4. Cover pan and steam for 20 minutes.

5. Uncover and flake rice with a fork from sides of pan. Mix in any milk that has not yet been absorbed.

6. Cover again and cook 5 more minutes. Serve hot with Jingha Molee or other curries.

.99¢
.99¢
.99¢
.99¢
ABOUT   .99¢
$1.99

Lentils in Garlic 4 SERVINGS

The myth of soaking dried lentils overnight has been exposed. So many recipes call for this and what usually ends up occurring is a mushy mess. My friend Whitney gets credit for this brilliant tidbit. This is a rare vegan addition, for my dear friends Valerie and Jack.

1½ cups Premiere lentils

1 cup Spice Box dried chopped onions (use fresh onions when available)

1 teaspoon Classic chopped garlic

6 tablespoons Imperial margarine, or butter

2½ cups hot water

Spice Supreme salt and pepper to taste

1 teaspoon El Pique ground cumin

1. Rinse lentils in cold water.

2. Soak dried onions in hot water for 5 to 10 minutes. Drain.

3. In a large saucepan, fry onions and garlic in margarine until soft.

4. Add lentils and stir for several minutes.

5. Add 2½ cups hot water; season with salt, pepper, and cumin.

6. Cover and simmer gently until done, about 1 hour. Serve with a dash of Master's lemon juice if desired.

continued on facing page

Lentils in Garlic CONTINUED

VARIATION

One of my favorite restaurants serves a similar version of these lentils, and I love it.

1. Cook the lentils al dente.

2. Drain and add them to the sautéed onions, garlic, and spices over high heat.

3. Add 1 can cooked ham, chopped, and flash-fry until ham is browned and lentils are crispy yet tender.

helpful hint

Dried lentils can serve as pie weights. When baking an unfilled crust, place a piece of foil in the center and add a handful of dried lentils (or bean of your choice) on top. Bake as directed, and this way your crust won't puff up and crack.

ABOUT
$2.99

Spinach Soufflé with Béchamel Sauce 6 SERVINGS

This soufflé is a delightful side to accompany Chicken Bundles (see "Main Courses"), but can also be presented as a main course itself for a light luncheon.

BÉCHAMEL SAUCE

2 tablespoons Danish Creamery butter

2 tablespoons Best Yet all-purpose flour, or 1 tablespoon plus 1 teaspoon Manischewitz cake meal

1 cup Springfresh milk

Spice Supreme salt and pepper to taste

Spice Box nutmeg to taste

1. In a saucepan over moderate heat, melt butter without browning.

2. Whisk in flour until well blended. Remove from heat.

3. In a separate saucepan, bring milk almost to the boiling point.

4. While stirring the flour mixture vigorously, add the hot milk all at once.

5. Bring back to a boil and allow to thicken.

6. Turn down heat and simmer for a few minutes—5 maximum.

7. Season with salt, pepper, and nutmeg.

continued on facing page

Spinach Soufflé with Béchamel Sauce CONTINUED

SOUFFLÉ

1 cup Béchamel sauce (recipe on previous page)

1 cup Kraft cheddar cheese, grated

½ teaspoon Heinz Worcestershire sauce

1 cup C&W frozen spinach, thawed, drained, and puréed

3 Country eggs, separated

1. Preheat oven to 400°F.

2. In a saucepan over medium low heat, combine Béchamel sauce, cheese, and Worcestershire sauce.

3. Stir until cheese is melted. Remove from heat. Add spinach.

4. In a grease-free bowl, beat egg whites until stiff but not dry.

5. In a separate bowl, beat the egg yolks until they are lemon-colored.

6. Add yolks to spinach mixture, and then gently fold in whites. (The more gently you incorporate the egg whites, the better your rise will be.)

7. Turn soufflé into a greased casserole dish and bake for about 30 minutes. The soufflé is done when a knife inserted in the center comes out clean.

helpful hint

Separating eggs is easiest when the egg is cold, but whites are best beaten at room temperature.

.99¢
.99¢
.99¢
.99¢
.99¢
.99¢
ABOUT
$6.99

Fried Rice 6 SERVINGS

The chicken and shrimp can be taken out of this recipe to make it vegetarian-friendly.

⅓ cup Spice Box dried chopped onions (use fresh onions when available)

1 tablespoon Bali's Best sweet-and-sour sauce

1 tablespoon Pearl River Bridge soy sauce

1 teaspoon Pure sesame oil

½ teaspoon water

McCormick pepper to taste

2 to 3 tablespoons Ideal vegetable oil for frying

½ cup Ready Pac coleslaw mix with carrots

1 cup Libby's sweet peas (optional, for color)

1 (5-ounce) can Crider chicken

2 (6-ounce) cans Sunny Sea shrimp pieces

5 ounces Orchid water chestnuts, sliced

3 cups Roberts A-1 white rice, cooked

2 Foremost eggs, slightly beaten

continued on facing page

helpful hint

1 cup of sesame oil mixed with 1 cup of Epsom salts will provide a distress soak for your tired bones—not to mention that your skin will end up glowing and well nourished.

62

Fried Rice CONTINUED

1. Soak dried onions in hot water for 5 to 10 minutes. Drain.

2. In a small bowl, blend sweet-and-sour sauce, soy sauce, sesame oil, water, and pepper and set aside.

3. Heat vegetable oil in a wok or pan.

4. Add drained onions, cabbage, and peas. Sauté until lightly browned.

5. Add chicken, shrimp, and water chestnuts and continue to sauté until heated through.

6. Reduce heat and add cooked rice and sweet-and-sour sauce mixture. Blend well.

7. Raise heat and add raw eggs, stirring constantly as you stir-fry.

8. Continue to fry until eggs are cooked through and rice is well mixed.

helpful hint

Let's set the record straight. Brown and white rice come form the same plant genus *Oryza*. What differentiates them is the amount of processing. If only the outer husk layer is removed then the rice will be categorized as brown. If after the husk, the next bran layer is also removed then the result will be white rice.

Processing is also responsible for the differences in black, white, and green teas. They all come from the same Camellia plant genus.

ABOUT
$3.99

Company Mashed Potatoes 6 SERVINGS

This dish calls specifically for instant potatoes, which makes it light, fluffy, and addictive!

4 cups Idaho Supreme instant mashed potatoes, prepared and hot

1 cup Knudsen sour cream

½ cup Encore dried chives

5 ounces Cheese Pleasers cheddar cheese, grated

½ teaspoon Chef's Choice garlic salt

1. Preheat oven to 350°F.

2. Combine potatoes, sour cream, chives, and cheese.

3. Place into a greased 1½-quart casserole dish. Sprinkle with garlic salt and bake until top is golden, about 25 minutes.

helpful hint

Out of garlic salt? Three parts salt to one part garlic powder will do just fine.

.99¢
.99¢
.99¢
.99¢
.99¢
ABOUT
$5.99

Mississippi Black-Eyed Peas 4–6 SERVINGS

Served with Sweet Potato Biscuits (see following page), this makes a great main dish for a luncheon. Especially cozy on a cool day.

4 (15-ounce) cans Allens Dorman black-eyed peas

2 cups water

¾ cup Spice Box dried chopped onions, reconstituted (use fresh onions when available)

1 (5-ounce) can Libby's cooked diced ham

McCormick salt and pepper to taste

1. Combine ingredients in a saucepan.

2. Bring to a slow boil, stirring often.

3. Reduce heat and simmer 20 minutes, stirring often to make sure there is no sticking. Serve hot.

helpful hint

Down on your luck? Maybe you're not eating enough black-eyed peas. It's a Southern tradition to start each New Year off with of bowl of these scrumptious legumes, since they're believed to bring good luck.

ABOUT
$7.99

Ham Chowder with Sweet Potato Biscuits 8 SERVINGS

I love these biscuits! They are perfect with the Ham Chowder, making this a balanced and satisfying meal.

BISCUITS

continued on facing page

2½ cups Cinch pancake mix

⅓ cup Imperial margarine, softened

1 cup S&W candied yams, rinsed, drained, and mashed

½ cup Springfresh milk

CHOWDER

1 (15-ounce) can Libby's whole white potatoes, mashed

1 (10½-ounce) can Baron cream of chicken soup

1 (15-ounce) can Libby's corn

1 cup Libby's cooked diced ham

1 (15-ounce) can Veg-All mixed vegetables

1¾ cups Springfresh milk

helpful hint

Since canned foods tend to settle while sitting on the shelf, opening from the bottom makes it easier to remove the contents.

Ham Chowder with
Sweet Potato Biscuits CONTINUED

1. Preheat oven to 450°F.

2. For the biscuits: Mix all ingredients until a soft dough forms.

3. Place dough on a flour-dusted surface and roll to coat.

4. Shape into a ball and knead four times.

5. Roll to one-half-inch thick. Cut with a 2½" cutter dipped in pancake mix to avoid sticking.

6. Place biscuits with edges touching on an ungreased cookie sheet. Bake for 10 to 12 minutes, until golden brown.

7. While biscuits are baking, combine all chowder ingredients in a nonstick frying pan over medium high heat and cook until heated through, about 10 minutes.

8. Place chowder in serving bowls and top with 2 biscuits. Serve hot.

helpful hint

In the United States, the terms yams and sweet potatoes are used interchangeably but in truth, they are very different. They may both be roots, but a yam comes from the yam family and needs hot moist weather to thrive. Sweet potatoes are from the morning glory family and are more abundant in the States, since they can withstand the colder weather. The USDA requires foods with "yam" on the label to be followed by the term "sweet potato." Chances are, unless you have specially sought out a yam at an international market, you probably have never eaten one.

Orange-Spiced Yams/Sweet Potatoes 6 SERVINGS

I have made a version of this dish (doused with sherry) every year for Thanksgiving up in Northern California. Chopped nuts, such as walnuts or almonds, can be added before baking if desired. Slicing the yams is aesthetically pleasing, since it sets this dish apart from the other holiday sides that are mashed or blended.

2 (16-ounce) cans S&W candied yams or 1 (29-ounce) can Princess sweet potatoes

¼ cup Mr. Toon's orange juice

2 tablespoons Fancy Choice pancake syrup

2 tablespoons Hartford House cornstarch

¼ cup water

2 teaspoons Spice Box dried parsley

½ cup Champion raisins (optional)

1. Heat oven to 400°F.

2. Drain and reserve liquid from yams, slice into rounds, and place yams in a greased baking dish.

3. Combine reserved liquid, orange juice, and syrup in a large saucepan and heat to a boil.

4. Mix cornstarch with water, then whisk into the sauce. Heat until thick enough to coat the back of a spoon. Remove from heat.

5. Add raisins to sauce, pour over yams, and bake for 25 minutes. Remove and garnish with parsley.

helpful hint

Mix together ¼ cup cornstarch and 2 cups cold water. Bring to a boil; boil until the mixture becomes thick. Pour into several small containers and add food coloring to each container. Voilà! You've created a collection of homemade finger paints.

.99¢
.99¢
.99¢
.99¢
.99¢
ABOUT
$4.99

Spinach Loaf with Creole Sauce 6 SERVINGS

Here's another side that can serve as a main dish for a luncheon or light dinner when accompanied by a soup such as Maine Corn Chowder (see recipe in this section).

2 tablespoons Spice Box dried onions (use fresh onions when available)

2 cups C&W cooked frozen spinach, thawed with the water squeezed out

2 Country eggs, well beaten

¾ cup Kraft cheddar bacon cheese, grated

1 cup Baker's Harvest cracker crumbs

1 tablespoon Citrovita red wine vinegar

4 slices Branding Iron bacon, cooked and diced, plus 2 tablespoons drippings

2 tablespoons Best Yet flour or Cinch pancake mix

1 cup Sun Roma diced tomatoes

2 tablespoons Food Club green chiles, diced

Spice Supreme salt and pepper to taste

1. Preheat oven to 350°F.

2. Soak dried onions in hot water for 5 to 10 minutes. Drain.

3. Blend spinach, eggs, cheese, crumbs, vinegar, and bacon drippings. Pour in baking dish and bake for 25 to 30 minutes.

4. In a medium saucepan, make Creole sauce by combining the bacon, onions, flour, tomatoes, chiles, salt, and pepper. Heat through and serve with spinach loaf.

helpful hint

An egg carton is a brilliant way to keep sewing or small workbench needs organized. I have one filled with buttons and another with screws and washers.

.99¢
.99¢
.99¢
.99¢
.99¢
ABOUT
$3.99

Tomato Corn Soup ABOUT 2 QUARTS

So great with grilled cheese sandwiches.

2 (13¾-ounce) cans Sweet Sue chicken broth

1 (1-pound) can Sun Roma tomatoes, chopped

1 (12-ounce) can Libby's corn

¼ teaspoon El Pique dried oregano or menudo spice mix

¼ teaspoon Spice Supreme salt and pepper

1. Combine all ingredients in a large saucepan.

2. Bring to a boil.

3. Reduce heat and simmer, covered, for 10 minutes. Serve hot.

helpful hint

When the folding tables come out, prevent them from separating by putting adjacent legs into a can. With a tablecloth over them, the tables will look and act like one continuous table, allowing nothing to fall between the seams.

.99¢
.99¢
.99¢
.99¢
.99¢
ABOUT
$3.99

Swamp Cabbage Salad with Spicy Dressing 4 SERVINGS

This is a spinoff of an old Seminole Indian recipe and is a great addition to barbecues.

3 (14-ounce) cans California Girl hearts of palm

1½ cups Banquet mayonnaise

2 to 3 tablespoons Citrovita apple cider vinegar

Spice Supreme salt and pepper to taste

1 tablespoon Encore dried chives

1 tablespoon Encore dried parsley

2 to 3 tablespoons Louisiana Select hot sauce

1. Rinse and drain hearts of palm well.

2. In a bowl, whisk together remaining ingredients.

3. Pour over hearts of palm and refrigerate at least 1 hour before serving.

helpful hint

Brighten up dull, lifeless hair by rinsing with 1 cup apple cider vinegar in 2 cups water after shampooing.

.99¢
.99¢
.99¢
.99¢
.99¢
ABOUT
$2.99

Tomato Pudding 4-6 SERVINGS

Don't get this confused with our American definition. My English grandmother was always making savory "puddings" that baffled me as a youngster. In my world, pudding was chocolate or it wasn't pudding. This is a nice sweet/savory dish, which is lighter than a bread and denser than a soufflé. It is a "pudding," and my friend Michael loves it!

1½ cups Lucky brown sugar

½ teaspoon McCormick salt

½ cup water

20 ounces California Healthy Harvest tomato purée

2 cups Premium white bread, trimmed and cut in squares

¾ cup Imperial margarine, melted

1. Preheat oven to 375°F.

2. In a saucepan, bring sugar, salt, water, and tomato purée to a boil.

3. Stir well and remove from heat.

4. Place bread squares at the bottom of a greased 13" × 9" baking dish.

5. Pour margarine over the bread, then pour the tomato mixture on top.

6. Bake for 45 minutes. Serve warm.

helpful hint

A slice of apple placed in a container of hardened brown sugar will soften it back up.

.99¢
.99¢
.99¢
.99¢
.99¢
ABOUT
$3.99

Spicy Sesame Noodles 10 SERVINGS

These are so simple, light, delicious, and affordable! With recipes like this, we can all eat and be merry! Prepare at least a day before serving so that the flavors can infuse the noodles.

2 pounds Long Life instant Chinese noodles

½ cup Pure sesame oil

½ cup Pearl River soy sauce

3 tablespoons Luv Yu rice vinegar

3 tablespoons Spreckels sugar

1½ teaspoons McCormick salt

2 tablespoons Orchid's chile oil

½ cup Encore dried chives

1. Cook noodles in a large pot of boiling water, one pound at a time.

2. Boil 4 to 5 minutes until tender.

3. Drain and rinse under cold water until noodles are thoroughly cooled. Drain and place in a large bowl.

4. Mix the rest of the ingredients together and let sit for 10 minutes so that the chives can reconstitute.

5. Using your hands, mix the sauce in with the noodles until noodles are well coated. Refrigerate overnight.

helpful hint

Adding a teaspoon of olive oil to cooking pasta can help prevent the water from boiling over.

Main Courses

.99¢
.99¢
.99¢
.99¢
.99¢

ABOUT
$3.99

Frittata Italiana 4 SERVINGS

Frittatas are great at all times of the day and are often served at room temperature, making them a great buffet item. Feel free to exchange the ham and cheese with ingredients of your choice. Adding all the ingredients to the egg mixture before cooking will save time and result in the ingredients being more integrated rather than layered. The choice is yours.

½ cup Autumn Gold mushroom pieces, rinsed and drained

3 tablespoons Danish Creamery butter

6 Foremost eggs, beaten

3 tablespoons HyVee evaporated milk, or cream substitute

McCormick salt and pepper to taste

2 tablespoons Spice Box parsley

2 tablespoons Aquilla Parmesan cheese

1 tablespoon Carapelli olive oil

1 can Hormel ham

Few drops of Master's lemon juice

4 ounces Whitehall Specialties American cheese

continued on facing page

helpful hint

An egg too short? One egg may be extended to two by adding 2 tablespoons of milk and ½ teaspoon of baking powder before scrambling.

Frittata Italiana CONTINUED

1. Preheat oven to 450°F.

2. Sauté mushrooms lightly in 1 tablespoon of the butter and set aside.

3. In a bowl, mix the eggs, milk, salt, pepper, parsley, and 1 tablespoon of Parmesan cheese.

4. Heat the olive oil and 1 tablespoon of butter in an ovenproof frying pan until butter turns white.

5. Pour in the egg mixture and cook over low heat until mixture is firm on the bottom but still soft on top, about 10 minutes. Remove from heat.

6. Sprinkle the top with mushrooms, ham, remaining Parmesan, lemon juice, cheese and remaining melted butter.

7. Place frying pan in oven and bake until cheese has melted, about 4 minutes or until top is firm, not runny. Remove to a hot platter and serve hot or at room temperature.

helpful hints

Think outside the ice-box! Frittatas are perfect vehicles for dinner leftovers. Have some extra steamed veggies? Throw 'em in. Shred that left over steak and add it too. Feel like something light? A frittata, like its omelet cousin, can be easily made with egg whites only. If a certain someone is resistant to this lighter preparation, you can add curry or saffron and your dish will not only taste delicious but its yellow color will leave them none the wiser.

.99¢
.99¢
.99¢
.99¢
.99¢
.99¢

ABOUT
$10.99

Vegetables in Coconut Gravy 6 SERVINGS

Feel free to pick the vegetables you prefer for this recipe. Depending on the tastes of your guests or the season, this dish can be prepared with many variations (Libby's mixed vegetables plus bamboo shoots, water chestnuts, carrots, potatoes, beets, peas, green beans works nicely). This is also vegetarian-friendly.

1 cup Spice Box dried chopped onions (use fresh onions when available)

2 to 3 (16 once) cans mixed vegetables, rinsed and drained

2 tablespoons Pure sesame oil

2 teaspoons Classic minced garlic

1 teaspoon El Pique crushed red chile pepper flakes

½ teaspoon Master's lemon juice

½ cup Hunt's whole tomatoes, chopped

2 cups ShariAnn's organic vegetable broth

1½ cups Thai Orchid coconut milk

3 teaspoons Pica creamy peanut butter

2 teaspoons Baja Pacific salt, or to taste

continued on facing page

helpful hint

Clean cans and remove labels. Fill with water and freeze. Use a drill or an ice pick to create a design of small holes around each can. Discard ice and place a tea light inside can. The patterns will bounce around and add to a lovely evening.

78

Vegetables in Coconut Gravy CONTINUED

1. Soak dried onions in hot water for 5 to 10 minutes. Drain and set aside.

2. Rinse and drain vegetables and cut into bite-size pieces.

3. In a medium saucepan, heat oil and fry onions until golden.

4. Add garlic and chiles and fry for about 2 minutes.

5. Add lemon juice and tomatoes. Stir and cook until pulpy.

6. Add broth and coconut milk and bring to a simmer, uncovered.

7. Add vegetables and heat through. They should all be tender yet crisp. When desired texture is achieved, stir in peanut butter and salt.

8. Serve with coconut rice, sliced bananas, and/or naan.

helpful hint

Coconuts may be cleaning up your act. The majority of water filters used domestically employ charcoal medium carbon, which is derived from the coconut husk.

.99¢
.99¢
.99¢
.99¢
ABOUT *.99¢*
$6.99

Spanish Toast 4 SERVINGS

Spanish Toast is something my mother would make for breakfast when friends slept over. It is an easy breakfast casserole. This is the basic recipe, but I know one of the reasons my mother liked to make it was that anything that needed to be used up could get thrown in.

1 cup Spice Box dried chopped onions (use fresh onions when available)

2 to 3 tablespoons Danish Creamery Butter

1 (6-ounce) can Mela large olives, chopped

6 Country eggs, hardboiled

½ pound Whitehall Specialties American cheese, grated

1 (8-ounce) bottle La Victoria taco sauce

1 loaf Premium white bread, toasted

Springfresh milk, for dipping

1. Preheat oven to 350°F.

2. Soak dried onions in hot water for 5 to 10 minutes. Drain.

3. Sauté onions in butter and set aside. In a medium bowl, combine the olives, eggs, cheese, and onions.

4. Heat taco sauce mixed with enough water to create a medium thick consistency.

5. In a greased baking dish, place a layer of toasted bread dipped in milk.

6. Spread egg mixture over toast and top with about ⅓ cup of the sauce. Top with another layer of milk-dipped toast and the rest of the sauce.

7. Bake for about 15 minutes. Serve hot.

helpful hint

I always save the remains of "dead" candles. When enough accumulate, I melt them down and use a cleaned out milk carton as a mold. It's amazing how many candles get remade this way.

.99¢
.99¢
.99¢
.99¢
.99¢

ABOUT
$2.99

Toad in the Hole 6 SERVINGS

This is Yorkshire pudding with sausages nestled inside. Using the cake meal will produce a denser, doughier dish; for a high rise, use flour or the pancake mix. Served with Green Beans au Gratin (see "Sides and Soups" section), this is a nourishing, economical supper.

1 pound (2 packages) Farmer John small fresh sausage links

2 tablespoons water

2 Country eggs

1 cup Springfresh milk

⅝ cup Manischewitz cake meal or 1 cup Cinch pancake mix, sifted

½ teaspoon Spice Supreme salt

Spice Supreme pepper to taste

1. Preheat oven to 425°F.

2. Place sausages and water in a frying pan. Cover and cook over low heat for 3 minutes.

3. Remove cover; increase heat to medium. Cook until water evaporates and sausages begin to brown. Set sausages aside, reserving the drippings.

4. In a large bowl, beat eggs with a mixer and slowly incorporate milk; blend well.

5. Add cake meal or pancake mix, salt, and pepper, mixing until batter is smooth.

6. Pour ¼ cup of the sausage drippings in bottom of an 11" × 7" × 1½" baking dish. Arrange sausage in dish and pour batter over all. Bake for 30 minutes.

helpful hint

Boiling sausage 5 to 10 minutes before frying can help reduce shrinkage and remove excess fat.

.99¢
.99¢
.99¢
.99¢
.99¢
ABOUT
$1.99

Salmon Soufflé with Hollandaise Sauce 3 SERVINGS

Canned salmon seems to always be available. It has a fishier taste than the fresh version, and you may want to take this into consideration when preparing salmon recipes. In this recipe, the Hollandaise sauce creates a perfect balance of flavors.

3 tablespoons Danish Creamery butter

3 tablespoons Cinch pancake mix

1 cup Springfresh milk

4 Foremost eggs, separated

Baja Pacific sea salt to taste

Heinz Worcestershire sauce to taste

1 cup Bay Beauty canned salmon

1. Preheat oven to 375°F.

2. Melt butter in a saucepan, stir in pancake mix, and blend with a whisk.

3. Meanwhile, bring the milk to a boil and add all at once to butter mixture, stirring until thick and smooth. Let mixture cool.

4. Beat in egg yolks, one at a time. Season with salt and Worcestershire sauce.

5. Flake salmon and add to the mixture.

6. With an electric mixer, beat egg whites until they stand in peaks. Be careful not to overbeat or they will become dry.

7. Fold whites gently into the salmon mixture, being careful not to overblend.

8. Pour into a 2-quart soufflé dish, greased or ungreased.

9. Place in oven and bake for 30 to 40 minutes.

10. Serve with Hollandaise sauce (recipe follows).

Salmon Soufflé with Hollandaise Sauce CONTINUED

ABOUT
$0.99

HOLLANDAISE SAUCE

3 Foremost egg yolks

1 tablespoon cold water

½ cup Danish Creamery butter, softened

¼ teaspoon Baja Pacific sea salt

½ teaspoon Master's lemon juice, or to taste

1. In a double boiler, combine egg yolks and water. Beat with a wire whisk over hot (not boiling) water until fluffy.

2. Add a few spoonfuls of the butter and beat until butter melts and sauce has started to thicken. Continue adding butter bit by bit, stirring constantly.

3. Add salt and lemon juice. Remove from heat and serve.

helpful hint

What to do with the whites? Give yourself a facial. Brush the egg whites on to the oily parts of skin. Allow yourself to be supine for at least 15 minutes. Rinse with warm water. Your face will be firm and nourished.

.99¢
.99¢
.99¢
.99¢
.99¢
ABOUT
$2.99

Curried Tuna Salad 4 SERVINGS

Curry goes so well with seafood. This combination was quite popular when I was young and is a delicious way to add some pizazz to a staple of the American diet. I am a big "sweet and savory" fan, so the raisins are a great part of this for me, but if you like to keep your tastes separate, feel free to omit them.

3 tablespoons Spice Box dried chopped onions (use fresh onions when available)

2 (6-ounce) cans Chicken of the Sea tuna, drained

1 tablespoon Encore dried parsley

1 tablespoon Champion golden raisins, plumped in 2 tablespoons warm water for 10 minutes.

2 teaspoons Albergo canola/olive oil blend

2 teaspoons Spice Box curry powder

¾ cup Banquet mayonnaise

McCormick salt and pepper to taste

½ teaspoon ReaLime lime juice, or more to taste

1. Soak dried onions in hot water for 5 to 10 minutes. Drain.

2. In a large bowl, break up tuna. Mix in onion, parsley, and raisins.

3. In a sauté pan, heat the oil over medium heat. Add the curry powder and stir until fragrant, about 30 seconds. Remove from heat and let cool.

4. Add curry oil to the mayonnaise; season with salt, pepper, and lime juice.

5. Gently mix the tuna with the seasoned mayonnaise. Serve in a sandwich, with crackers, or on a bed of lettuce.

helpful hint

An empty tuna can is perfect to use as an egg poacher. Remove the bottom of the can as well as the top and remove any paper label. Then place the metal ring in a frying pan of simmering water, and crack an egg into it.

.99¢
.99¢
.99¢
.99¢
.99¢
ABOUT
$2.99

Tuna and Rice Soufflé 6 SERVINGS

Tuna is readily available at my favorite store. I wanted to show how it can be used in different ways. A soufflé is always a crowd pleaser, and it seems that savory ones are due for a comeback.

1 (10-ounce) can Marie Callender's condensed cream of mushroom soup

1 (6-ounce) can Smiling Sea tuna, drained and flaked

1 cup Robert's A-1 rice, cooked

¼ cup Dromedary pimientos, chopped

2 tablespoon Encore dried parsley

4 Country eggs

1. Preheat oven to 350°F.

2. Heat and stir soup in a saucepan.

3. Add tuna, rice, pimiento, and parsley; heat through. Remove from heat.

4. Separate eggs. Beat whites until stiff.

5. Beat yolks until thick and lemon-colored; gradually stir in tuna mixture.

6. Pour slowly onto beaten egg whites, folding together gently yet thoroughly.

7. Turn into an ungreased 2-quart casserole. Bake for 30 to 35 minutes or until set in center. Serve immediately.

helpful hint

A clean, label-free tuna can is a great mold for mini holiday gift cakes. Just grease and fill with batter. Adjust baking time if necessary.

.99¢
.99¢
.99¢
.99¢
.99¢

ABOUT
$6.99

Green Chile Torte 2 SERVINGS FOR A MAIN COURSE, 8 HORS D'OEUVRES

I found this recipe in the chipped avocado-green recipe box that was passed on to me. A fad in the 1970s was stationary with one's name in a funky font at the top. In this case, my Aunt Connie's name was at the top. The paper had been opened and folded so many times it practically dissolved in my hands. I am happy to be able to transcribe it here for posterity.

4 (4-ounce) cans Food Club Mexican style green chiles

6 Guerrero corn tortillas

Gold-N-Sweet vegetable oil for frying

McCormick salt and pepper to taste

8 (1-ounce) Tiger Switzerland Gruyère cheese wedges diced, or 1½ cups preferred cheese shredded or diced.

1 (10½-ounce) can Baron cream of mushroom soup

1 cup Springfresh milk

Louisiana Gem hot sauce

1. Preheat oven to 350°F.

2. Drain chiles in strainer.

3. Fry tortillas lightly in oil; season with salt and pepper

4. In a 9" square baking dish, place two tortillas side by side slightly overlapping the inside edges, and top with a layer of chiles and cheese. Repeat layers with remaining tortillas, chiles, and cheese.

5. Mix soup, milk, and salt and pepper to taste. Pour over layered tortillas and bake for 35 to 45 minutes. Cool, garnish with hot sauce, and slice into triangles.

helpful hint

Quartering some extra tortillas and frying them up in the already prepared oil will supply you and your guests with homemade chips while dinner is cooking.

.99¢
.99¢
.99¢
.99¢
.99¢

ABOUT
$8.99

Jhinga Molee 4 SERVINGS

Known as white curry in Sri Lanka, this is an extremely mild curry. The pan should not be covered at any time, and liquid should be stirred often to prevent the coconut milk from curdling.

1½ cups Spice Box dried chopped onions (use fresh onions when available)

1 tablespoon Danish Creamery butter

1 teaspoon Spice Box ginger powder

2½ teaspoons Classic minced garlic

2 Las Palmas whole green chiles, slit and seeded

1 teaspoon Spice Box turmeric

2 teaspoons Spice Box curry powder

1 (14-ounce) can Vanor coconut milk

1 teaspoon McCormick salt

4 (6-ounce) cans Sunny Sea broken shrimp, rinsed and picked over

Master's lemon juice to taste

1. Soak dried onions in hot water for 5 to 10 minutes. Drain.

2. Heat butter in a frying pan and fry onions, ginger, and garlic until barely golden.

3. Add chiles, turmeric, and curry powder; fry for 1 minute more.

4. Add the coconut milk and salt while bringing to a simmer. Simmer uncovered for 10 minutes, then add shrimp and cook 5 to 10 minutes.

5. Remove from heat and add lemon juice to taste. Serve over a bed of white rice.

helpful hint

Doubling a recipe does not mean doubling the seasonings, especially salt. Start by adding half the amount of additional seasonings and use your taste buds to gauge the extra salt (if any) that may be needed.

ABOUT
$4.99

.99¢
.99¢
.99¢
.99¢
.99¢

Macaroni and Cheese 4 SERVINGS

This recipe is a bit drier than the box version. I suppose you could consider it more of a casserole. I think my mother discovered this and liked it enough to stick with it because the only time I ate the box version was when I would go a friend's house. Try it—you'll like it.

6 ounces Allegra miniature elbow macaroni

¾ cup bread crumbs made from 1 loaf Premium white bread (as described) or ¾ cup Manischewitz matzo meal

4 tablespoons Imperial margarine

1 (10½-ounce) can Baron cream of mushroom soup

½ cup Springfresh milk

McCormick salt and pepper to taste

1 bottle Eazee Squeeze cheese sauce, or ½ pound any American or cheddar cheese from the refrigerator section, diced

Messana grated Parmesan cheese

continued on facing page

helpful hint

Need some help keeping the little ones still until lunch is ready? Cut some yarn and have them string together necklaces, bracelets, or anklets with the uncooked pasta. When they reach the desired length, tie the ends and color the pasta with non-toxic markers.

Macaroni and Cheese CONTINUED

1. Cook macaroni according to package directions.

2. Make bread crumbs by placing entire loaf of bread on oven rack at 200°F. Cook until bread is dry enough to crumble in your hands, about 30 minutes.

3. After removing bread, raise oven temperature to 350°F.

4. In a sauté pan, melt the margarine and sauté bread crumbs until margarine has all been absorbed. Set aside.

5. Combine soup, milk, salt, and pepper.

6. Place alternate layers of macaroni, soup mix, and cheese in a small greased baking dish. Top with bread crumbs and sprinkle with Parmesan cheese.

7. Bake for 35 to 45 minutes. Do not overbake or it will get too dry.

helpful hint

Measuring margarine from a tub can be daunting to those who rely on the increment marks that come pre-printed on sticks. If this happens, try using the displacement method. Fill a measuring cup with cold water to the point you do not want the margarine. Then add margarine until the water level reaches your desired amount. Con-fused? Basically if you need ⅔ cup of butter or margarine, fill the mea-suring cup with ⅓ cup cold water. Then add the fat until 1 full cup is reached.

.99¢
.99¢
.99¢
.99¢
.99¢
ABOUT
$4.99

Hawaiian Ham Pie 6–8 SERVINGS

This is a classic example of cooking circa 1967, created before I was born and proven to still be delicious today. I whipped this up and drove over to a friend's house in Venice, California, where six famished surfers proceeded to devour the pie. When they realized I had only brought one, the gentle giants began to whine and I quickly took my leave, reminding them that they were my tasters, not my children!

⅓ cup bread crumbs made from ½ loaf Premium white bread

2 tablespoons Savion sliced dried onions (use fresh onions when available)

1 Pastry for Savory Pie Crust (see recipe in "Baked Goods and Desserts")

2 (5-ounce) cans Libby's ham

1 (4-ounce) can Underwood deviled ham spread

1 Country egg, beaten

½ cup Springfresh milk

1 tablespoon Morehouse spicy brown mustard

1 (29-ounce) can Sun Giant crushed pineapple

½ cup Lucky golden brown sugar (optional)

continued on facing page

helpful hint

No more soggy crusts! As soon as the crust lines the pan, brush it with soft butter and refrigerate until the butter is firm. Add filling and proceed with cooking.

Hawaiian Ham Pie CONTINUED

1. Preheat oven to 350°F. You can use this time to prepare the bread crumbs if necessary. Be careful not to let the bread slices burn.

2. Soak dried onions in hot water for 5 to 10 minutes. Drain.

3. Prepare pastry according to recipe. Flatten ball on a lightly floured surface. Roll out to one-eighth-inch thick and form into an 8" or 9" pie tin. Trim edge to one-half inch past tin; fold under and flute.

4. Combine ham, ham spread, bread crumbs, egg, milk, onions, mustard, and ½ cup of the pineapple. Blend well. Spread into pastry shell.

5. In a small bowl, combine remaining pineapple and sugar. Arrange on top of ham in a spoke pattern. Bake for 45 minutes.

helpful hint

Hawaiian residents eat an average of 4 cans of SPAM per person, per year. If you're planning a trip to Waikiki in April, check out the annual Spam Jam, the street festival that celebrates the canned meat. The 2004 celebration boasted a 313 ft. musubi – an island snack best described as SPAM sushi.

.99¢
.99¢
.99¢
.99¢
.99¢
.99¢
ABOUT
$6.99

Chicken Bundles 6 SERVINGS

Since these are self-contained, they make a good buffet item. In the winter they could be served with a heartier side dish like Company Mashed Potatoes, and in warmer weather with dishes like Asian Soul Slaw or Swamp Cabbage Salad.

2½ cups Crider chopped cooked chicken

8 ounces Knudsen sour cream

¼ cup Banquet mayonnaise

¾ cup Veg-All canned vegetables

McCormick salt and pepper to taste

Pillsbury dough or Pizza crust dough (see recipe in this section)

1. Preheat oven to 375°F.

2. In a large bowl, combine all ingredients except the dough.

3. Divide dough into 12 equal parts.

4. For each bundle, roll out one portion of the dough onto a floured surface (use cake meal or pancake mix if necessary).

5. Place ¼ cup of the chicken mixture on one side of dough. Fold over other half and seal edges with a fork.

6. Place bundles in greased pan, cover, and let rest for 20 minutes. Prick with a fork and brush with some milk.

7. Bake for 20 to 25 minutes. Serve warm.

helpful hint

An egg wash can substitute for the brushed milk and will add color and shine to many of your baked goods. Beat together an egg yolk, white, or whole egg with 2 tablespoons of water and brush over the pastry before baking.

.99¢
.99¢
.99¢
.99¢
.99¢
ABOUT
$12.99

Mexican Chicken 6 SERVINGS

A layer of jalapeño slices and/or hot salsa will let you spice this up to your own taste. This can be prepared quickly, and if you freeze your cheese, all the ingredients can be kept in stock.

1 cup Spice Box dried chopped onions (use fresh onions when available)

2 to 3 tablespoons Dutch farms Wisconsin margarine

1 (10½-ounce) can Baron cream of mushroom soup

1 (10½-ounce) can Baron cream of chicken soup

1 (28-ounce) can Sun Roma sliced tomatoes

3 cups Crider cooked chicken

16 Guerrero corn tortillas, quartered

3 cups Cheese Pleasers grated cheese, jack or cheddar

1. Preheat oven to 350°F.

2. Soak dried onions in hot water for 5 to 10 minutes. Drain.

3. Sauté onions in margarine until golden.

4. In a large bowl, mix soups, tomatoes, and chicken. Mix in onions.

5. Line a baking dish with quartered tortillas, then chicken mixture, then cheese. Repeat layers, finishing off with cheese. Bake for 35 minutes.

helpful hint

If you use commercial products to clean your oven, be sure to cover the thermostat wire with newspaper or foil. Harsh cleaners throw off your cooking temperatures. Be sure to remove your covering after cleaning and before turning the oven on.

.99¢
.99¢
.99¢
.99¢
.99¢
ABOUT
$23.99

Chicken Tetrazzini 25 SERVINGS*

I have come across many different versions of this throughout the years. It is named after opera singer Luisa Tetrazzini. Playing one of her arias while dining makes this dish taste even more delizioso!

1 cup Spice Box dried chopped onions [¼ cup] (use fresh onions when available)

1½ pounds Allegra spaghetti [6 ounces]

1 teaspoon Classic crushed garlic [¼ teaspoon]

3 tablespoons Danish Creamery butter [1 tablespoon]

4 (10½-ounce) cans Baron cream of mushroom soup [1 can]

4 (10½-ounce) cans Baron cream of chicken soup [1 can]

2 teaspoons Heinz steak sauce [½ teaspoon]

4 cups Springfresh milk [1 cup]

1½ pounds Kraft sharp cheddar cheese, shredded [6 ounces]

12 (5-ounce) cans Crider cooked diced chicken [20 ounces]

2 cups Forrelli mushrooms, optional [½ cup]

4 ounces Dromedary pimientos, diced [1 ounce]

⅓ cup Encore dried parsley [pinch]

Spice Supreme pepper

Spice Box paprika

continued on facing page

*For 6 servings ($5.99), use amounts in brackets.

helpful hint

Placing pasta in a deep-fryer basket before submerging it into the pot of boiling water eliminates the need for a strainer and hot water mishaps.

Chicken Tetrazzini CONTINUED

1. Preheat oven to 375°F.

2. Soak dried onions in hot water for 10 minutes. Drain.

3. Cook and drain spaghetti. Rinse in hot water and set aside.

4. In a large frying pan sauté onions and garlic in butter.

5. Add soups, steak sauce, milk, and half the cheese. Cook until smooth, stirring frequently.

6. Add chicken, mushrooms (optional), pimientos, and parsley and mix well. Add pepper to taste.

7. Mix lightly with spaghetti. Place in one or two shallow baking dishes and sprinkle with remaining cheese and paprika. Bake for about 30 minutes.

helpful hints

This is the ultimate comfort food. Tuna or turkey can be substituted for a twist or simply because it's what you've got in the cupboard. Remember these recipes are meant to work for you.

.99¢
.99¢
.99¢
.99¢
.99¢
ABOUT
$16.99

Wedding Day Chicken Supreme 8–10 SERVINGS

Preparing this the day before allows for less stress and a clean kitchen when company arrives. I highly recommend this method. When time is scarce, being able to pop the dish into a preheated oven, and not have any cleanup, is a great help.

6 to 9 slices Oliver's country white bread, trimmed of crusts

9 (5-ounce) cans (4 cups) Libby's cooked chicken, diced

½ pound Autumn Gold sliced mushrooms

½ cup Dutch Farms Wisconsin margarine

8 ounces 4 Seasons water chestnuts, sliced

½ pound Kraft cheddar cheese, grated

4 Country eggs, well beaten

2 cups Springfresh milk

1 teaspoon Spice Supreme salt

1 (10½-ounce) can Baron cream of mushroom soup

1 (10½-ounce) can Baron cream of celery soup

1 (7-ounce) jar Dromedary pimientos, diced

2 cups Manischewitz matzo meal, sautéed with 3 tablespoons Danish Creamery butter

continued on facing page

helpful hint

Having water chestnuts on hand will give you the ability to add crunch and texture to soups, salads, stuffings, and more! Their mild taste makes them extremely versatile.

Wedding Day Chicken Supreme CONTINUED

1. Line a greased 10" × 14" baking dish with bread. Top with chicken.

2. Cook mushrooms in margarine for 2 to 3 minutes. Combine with water chestnuts and spoon over chicken. Top with cheese.

3. Combine eggs, milk, and salt and pour over chicken.

4. Mix soups and pimientos and spoon over all. Cover with foil and refrigerate overnight.

5. Bake uncovered at 350°F for 1¼ hours.

6. Remove from oven and sprinkle with matzo meal. Return to oven for 15 minutes. Let stand for 5 to 10 minutes before serving.

helpful hints

When was the last time you just sat in a park and took a few minutes for yourself? Use those cut off bread crusts as a catalyst. It may sound silly but feeding the birds and the squirrels can really renew one's outlook. Go on, give it a go.

.99¢
.99¢
.99¢
.99¢
.99¢
ABOUT
$9.99

Curried Chicken with Cashews 6 SERVINGS

Also known as Kaju Murgh Kari, this is a thick and flavorful curry that absolutely must be served with Naan (see "Baked Goods and Desserts") to soak up all the delicious sauce. Remember, long, slow cooking is key to a good curry. Long is relative here because the chicken is already cooked, but the base should be made with patient care.

1½ cups Spice Box dried chopped onions (use fresh onions when available)

3 tablespoon Danish Creamery butter

3 teaspoons Gilroy Farms minced garlic

1 teaspoon Spice Box ginger powder

3 tablespoons Spice Box curry powder

1 teaspoon Spice Box Mexican chili powder

3 teaspoons McCormick salt

1 cup Hunt's whole tomatoes, chopped

5 to 6 (5-ounce) cans Libby's chicken, rinsed and drained

2 teaspoons Encore Gourmet coriander powder

2 teaspoons McCormick pepper

½ teaspoon El Pique cumin seeds

2 Spice Box whole cloves

Dash of Spice Box nutmeg

Dash of Spice Supreme cinnamon

½ cup Dannon plain yogurt

4 ounces Star Snacks cashew pieces, finely chopped or ground

continued on facing page

helpful hint

An equal amount of sour cream or puréed cottage cheese can substitute for yogurt.

Curried Chicken with Cashews CONTINUED

1. Soak dried onions in hot water for 5 to 10 minutes. Drain.

2. Heat butter in a large saucepan. Gently fry onions, garlic, and ginger until golden.

3. Add curry and chili powders and stir 1 minute.

4. Add salt and tomatoes and cook to a rich pulp, stirring with a wooden spoon.

5. Add chicken, stirring well to coat. Cover and simmer for 5 minutes.

6. Stir in the rest of the spices and yogurt and simmer uncovered for a few minutes, stirring to ensure that the spices do not stick.

7. Stir in the cashews, heat through, and serve with chapatis, naan, or coconut rice.

helpful hint

More people are allergic to peanuts but cashews can trigger a worse reaction. So to ensure your dinner goes smoothly, it will behoove you to check with your guests before preparing this or any dish that contains nuts.

.99¢
.99¢
.99¢
.99¢
.99¢

ABOUT
$18.99

Salmon Potato Chip Casserole 25 SERVINGS

This recipe is great for a large group of people and can easily be made at the last minute. If you enjoy this kind of salmon, you will love this dish. The potato chips give it that "high class" touch.

1 cup Savion sliced dried onions (use fresh onions when available)

½ cup Imperial margarine

¼ cup Best Yet flour

5 (10½-ounce) cans Baron condensed cream of mushroom soup

1 quart Springfresh milk

5 (5-ounce) bags (12 cups) Olive Oil Potato Chips, coarsely crushed

5 (14¾-ounce) cans Prelate Keta salmon, drained and flaked

1½ (15-ounce) cans Green Giant tender sweet peas, drained

1. Preheat oven to 350°F.

2. Soak dried onions in hot water for 5 to 10 minutes. Drain.

3. In a 3-quart saucepan melt margarine. Add onions and cook but do not brown.

4. Blend in flour and stir until bubbly. Add soup and gradually add milk until smooth.

5. Set aside 2 cups of the crushed potato chips. Layer the remaining potato chips in two 13" x 9" x 2" baking pans; top with salmon, peas, and soup mixture.

6. Crumble reserved chips on top and bake 40 to 45 minutes until heated through.

helpful hint

To give your casserole dish new life:- Mix 3 teaspoons of vinegar and 3 teaspoons of cream of tartar and use a cotton ball to apply it to your casserole dishes. Let sit about 10 minutes. Scrub with a scouring pad and then wash in hot, soapy water.

.99¢
.99¢
.99¢
.99¢
.99¢
ABOUT
$2.99

Tuna Noodle Casserole 4 SERVINGS

Since this recipe is still alive and well after so many years, I felt it necessary to include it in the book. It's retro American cuisine at its best.

2 cups Allegra noodles or pasta of choice

2 (6-ounce) cans (1 cup) Chicken of the Sea tuna, drained

1 (10½-ounce) can Marie Callender's condensed cream of mushroom soup

1 teaspoon Heinz Worcestershire sauce

1 teaspoon Spice Box curry powder

10–20 Vista saltine crackers, crumbled

1. Preheat oven to 450°F.

2. Cook pasta according to package directions. Drain and set aside.

3. Separate tuna into large flakes.

4. Grease a medium-size ovenproof casserole dish. Layer pasta, then fish, until finished.

5. In a bowl, mix the soup, Worcestershire sauce, and curry powder. Pour over tuna and pasta.

6. Top casserole with cracker crumbs and bake until top is nicely browned.

helpful hint

Because the pasta in baked dishes is cooked twice—boiled first and then combined with other ingredients and cooked in the oven—the pasta in baked dishes should boil for less time than normal, about one-half to two-thirds the time.

.99¢
.99¢
.99¢
.99¢
ABOUT .99¢
$2.99

Spaghetti alla Carbonara 4 SERVINGS

This dish is quick, easy, and delicious. Bacon is the traditional ingredient and may be used if desired. If you are hesitant about the eggs cooking on their own, you can turn the heat on under the pot as you toss but be careful not to overcook!

8 ounces Allegra no. 8 spaghetti

1 (6-ounce) can Libby's chunks of ham or 6 ounces hot cooked diced bacon

2 Country eggs

3 ounces Messana brand Parmesan cheese

McCormick salt and pepper to taste

1. Cook spaghetti al dente.

2. While it is cooking, cook ham or bacon in a frying pan until browned and crisp separating into bits as it cooks. If using ham, heat through until slightly browned and crisp.

3. In a bowl, beat the eggs well. Add 2 ounces of Parmesan and season with salt and pepper.

4. When spaghetti is cooked, drain, return to pot quickly, and add egg mixture (the heat of the pasta is sufficient to cook the eggs).

5. Add ham or bacon, toss well, and serve immediately with remaining Parmesan.

helpful hint

Dried pasta doubles in volume when cooked. Measure dried pasta by weight and cooked pasta by volume.

.99¢
.99¢
.99¢
.99¢
.99¢
ABOUT
$6.99

Pasta con Sarde 4 SERVINGS

Sardines are something many people shy away from but are wonderful to keep in stock. They transform any dish from a bland staple to aromatic delicacy. Canned, they can be found marinated in oil, tomato sauce, mustard, or lemon juice. They improve with age and should be kept in a cool dry place. Do not refrigerate, for the oil then becomes solidified and stops the infusing process.

1 cup Spice Box dried chopped onions (use fresh onions when available)

⅓ cup Di Buon Gusto olive oil

4 Polar flat anchovies, drained, patted dry and minced

¼ cup toasted Star Snacks cashew bits

2 tablespoons Champion raisins, plumped in hot water for 10 minutes

3¾ ounces Royal Fish sardines packed in oil, drained

¾ pound Allegra pasta of choice

⅓ cup Manischewitz matzo meal

1. Soak dried onions in hot water for 5 to 10 minutes. Drain.

2. In a large frying pan, heat oil. Add onions and cook, stirring until golden.

3. Add anchovies and cook, stirring, over low heat until melted.

4. Add nuts, raisins, and sardines, stirring occasionally until heated through, about 5 minutes.

5. In a larger pot of boiling salted water, cook the pasta al dente. Drain.

6. Transfer to a serving bowl; add sardine mixture and bread crumbs. Toss to combine, and serve.

helpful hint

To keep your creation hot: Fill a heatproof serving bowl with boiling water and let stand until ready to use. Pour out the water and dry the bowl. Warmed plates can be prepared by placing them in a 200°F oven 10 minutes before serving.

.99¢
.99¢
.99¢
.99¢
.99¢
ABOUT
$4.99*

Pasta Pomodoro 6 SERVINGS

A great recipe for all. Excluding the chicken or shrimp and substituting vegetable broth makes this vegetarian-friendly. It is a hearty dinner served piping hot, but also a good main dish for a luncheon served at room temperature.

½ cup Spice Box dried chopped onions (use fresh onions when available)

16 ounces Allegra angel hair pasta

¼ cup Di Buon Gusto olive oil

4 teaspoons Classic crushed garlic

2 cups Sun Roma diced tomatoes

2 tablespoons Citrovita red wine/balsamic vinegar

1 (14.5-ounce) can Sweet Sue chicken broth

El Pique crushed red pepper to taste

Spice Supreme pepper

2 tablespoons Encore dried parsley

¼ cup Aquilla Parmesan cheese

2 (5-ounce) cans Crider cooked chicken or 2 (6-ounce) cans Sunny Sea shrimp pieces, rinsed and picked over (optional)

1. Soak dried onions in hot water for 10 minutes. Drain.

2. In a large pot of boiling water, cook pasta until al dente; drain and set aside.

3. In a large frying pan over high heat, pour olive oil. Add onions and garlic and cook until golden.

4. Reduce heat. Add tomatoes, vinegar, and broth; simmer for about 8 minutes.

5. Stir in red pepper, black pepper, parsley, and cooked pasta. Toss thoroughly. Simmer for 5 more minutes

6. Serve topped with Parmesan cheese. Chicken or shrimp pieces can be added to sauce right before pasta if desired.

*$6.99 w/chicken or shrimp.

helpful hint

Hot water (not cold) is the trick to "unsticky" spaghetti. The spaghetti can even sit in the water, but add some cold if not serving immediately to avoid overcooking. Then just rinse under hot water again right before serving.

ABOUT
$3.99

Pasta with Smoked Mussels and Capers 4 SERVINGS

Using capers to flavor seafood dishes has been traced back to the Romans. The pickled jar kind, which is what this recipe calls for, are sour and full of their own unique flavor, creating a perfect balance with the smoked mussels. All versions of canned sardines would work well in this recipe—use whichever suits your fancy.

8 ounces Allegra elbow macaroni

3 to 4 ounces Sunny Sea smoked mussels or oysters, drained

2½ ounces Royal Fish smoked sardines, packed in oil

1 tablespoon Sunny Harvest capers

Handful of Encore dried parsley

2 tablespoons Master's lemon juice (use fresh lemons when available)

2 tablespoons Di Buon Gusto olive oil

Spice Supreme salt

El Pique crushed red pepper flakes

¼ cup Encore dried chives

1. Prepare pasta according to package directions.

2. Coarsely chop mussels, sardines, and capers. Place in a mixing bowl.

3. Add parsley, lemon juice, and olive oil. Season to taste with salt and red pepper.

4. When pasta is done, drain and add to the mixing bowl. Toss with chives, reserving some for garnish. Serve warm.

helpful hint

Capers and their juice can be used in place of olives in dry and dirty martinis.

.99¢
.99¢
.99¢
.99¢
.99¢
ABOUT
$3.99

Steak Dianne 2 SERVINGS

This is a rarer possibility, since steak is not always available. I wanted to include it to show how lavish one can be with good timing and an open mind.

3 tablespoons Savion dried sliced onions (use fresh onions when available)

2 (4-ounce) American Companies beef rib-eye steaks

½ teaspoon Spice Supreme salt

½ teaspoon Spice Supreme pepper

6 tablespoons Danish Creamery butter

1 teaspoon Grey Poupon Dijon mustard

1 tablespoon Master's lemon juice

1½ teaspoons Heinz Worcestershire sauce

½ teaspoon Classic crushed garlic

¾ cup water mixed with ¼ cup Aunt Nellie's beef gravy

3 ounces Forrelli mushrooms, drained

¼ cup Christian Brothers white brandy or ½ cup dry white wine (I used Prosperity)

2 tablespoons Encore dried parsley

continued on facing page

helpful hint

Two teaspoons of Dijon mustard will really jazz up an otherwise ordinary oil-and-vinegar salad dressing.

Steak Dianne CONTINUED

1. Soak dried onions in hot water for 5 to 10 minutes. Drain.

2. Season steaks with salt and pepper and refrigerate for 1 hour.

3. Melt 3 tablespoons butter in a frying pan. Add the mustard and 2 tablespoons of the onions. Sauté for 1 minute over medium-high heat.

4. Add steaks and brown for about 3 to 4 minutes each side (until medium-rare). Remove steaks to a platter and keep warm.

5. Add remaining butter, lemon juice, Worcestershire sauce, garlic, remaining onion and the water gravy mixture to the pan drippings. Cook for about 2 minutes, then add mushrooms and brandy or wine.

6. Boil, stirring frequently, until gravy is reduced to about ½ cup. Pour over steaks, sprinkle with parsley, and serve.

helpful hints

Legend has it that an English lord became a great fan of a special sauce while living in India. When he returned he sought out to have it replicated but the result was considered a failure and banned to the basement. A few years later it was tasted again and its fermentation had turned it into something delicious. In 1883 Worcestershire Sauce was introduced to the public.

.99¢
.99¢
.99¢
.99¢
.99¢
.99¢
ABOUT
$9.99

Jambalaya 6–8 SERVINGS

The chicken and ham in this recipe can be substituted with shrimp, crab, mussels, or clams in the same proportions for a totally different taste. The Pique Menudo spice mix can be added to taste if you are looking to spice things up.

1 cup Spice Box dried chopped onions (use fresh onions when available)

2 tablespoons Rex lard

3 teaspoons Classic crushed garlic

2 packages (16 total) Farmer John small uncooked pork sausage links

2 (5-ounce) cans Hormel cooked ham

2 (5-ounce) cans Crider cooked chicken

2½ cups Hunt's diced tomatoes, undrained

1 cup Robert's A-1 white rice, uncooked

1½ cups Sweet Sue chicken broth

½ teaspoon Spice Box ground sage

1 tablespoon Encore dried parsley

1 teaspoon Spice Box Mexican chili powder

1½ teaspoons Spice Supreme salt

1 teaspoon Spice Supreme pepper

1. Preheat oven to 350°F.

2. Soak dried onions in hot water for 5 to 10 minutes. Drain.

3. Melt lard in a frying pan and sauté onions and garlic until golden.

4. Add the sausage and break up while stirring. Add ham and chicken and cook for 5 minutes.

5. Add the tomatoes with their liquid, rice, broth, sage, parsley, chili powder, salt, and pepper.

6. Turn mixture into a casserole dish. Cover and bake until rice is tender, about 45 minutes.

helpful hint

For a dish such as this, oil or butter can substitute for the lard. For pie crusts, however, only vegetable shortening will come close to achieving the same flakiness.

.99¢
.99¢
.99¢
.99¢
.99¢
ABOUT
$10.99

Turkey Tostadas 6 SERVINGS

Mexican-influenced food always seems to please. Its appealing trait is that one can add all sorts of ingredients to personalize the dish. Look for sour cream, guacamole, or salsa fresca in the refrigerator section. They all make great additions, and, set out in separate bowls, allow your guests to have their tostadas exactly how they want them. And don't forget the Tabasco!

12 Guerrero corn tortillas

Gold-N-Sweet vegetable oil for frying

4 cups Diamond A refried beans

2 cups Kraft cheddar bacon cheese, shredded

2 cups Libby's canned turkey

3 cups Ready Pac shredded coleslaw mix with carrots

1 cup Sun Roma diced tomatoes

1 (8-ounce) bottle La Victoria taco sauce

1. Fry tortillas in half an inch of hot oil until crisp (about 3 seconds), pressing each tortilla under oil with a spatula. Remove and drain on paper towels.

2. Heat beans in a saucepan and spread on tortillas.

3. Layer with cheese, turkey, cabbage, and tomatoes. Top with taco sauce. Serve warm.

helpful hint

Tortillas can be fried in advance, stored in an airtight container, and heated in a 300°F oven before you construct the tostadas. This will cut down preparation and cleanup before your guests arrive.

.99¢
.99¢
.99¢
.99¢
.99¢
ABOUT
$2.99

Corned Beef Casserole 4 SERVINGS

This, like most casseroles, can be doubled easily. It is hearty and makes great leftovers. At about $0.75 per serving, it is a tasty way to get through a financially trying week.*

1 tablespoon Spice Box dried chopped onions (use fresh onions when available)

1 cup Allegra macaroni

1 (12-ounce) can Clasico corned beef

1 (15-ounce) can Libby's cream-style corn

¼ cup Spice Box dried chives

1. Preheat oven to 350°F.

2. Soak dried onions in hot water for 5 to 10 minutes. Drain.

3. Cook macaroni according to package instructions. Drain.

4. In a mixing bowl, break up corned beef; add onions, corn, and chives.

5. Mix in macaroni and place in a medium-size greased casserole dish. Bake until golden and bubbly, about 30 minutes.

*Note: This dish can be prepared the night before and refrigerated before baking. Bring to room temperature before placing in oven.

helpful hint

Pasta added to water before it starts to boil can become mushy. The heat of boiling water seals the outside of the pasta, preventing it from sticking together.

ABOUT
$2.99

Easter "Ham" Drizzled with Raisin Cider Sauce 4 SERVINGS

Canned meats such as Spam are looked upon in America as being slightly low-class. In parts of Europe, however, it is still a popular staple. Being creative makes all the difference. In this case, the sauce was the inspiration for this recipe. It is a lovely and aromatic glaze. Gingered Beets (in the "Sides and Soups" section) would be a nice side dish with this.

2 (12-ounce) cans Spam ham or Royale chicken loaf

SAUCE

¼ cup Lucky brown sugar

1½ tablespoons Hartford House cornstarch

⅛ teaspoon Spice Supreme salt

1 cup Citrovita apple cider vinegar

¼ cup Champion raisins

8 Spice Box whole cloves

1 tablespoon Dutch Wisconsin Farms margarine

Dash of Spice Supreme cinnamon to taste

1. Mix sugar and cornstarch in a saucepan.

2. Add remaining sauce ingredients and cook over medium heat, stirring constantly, until raisins are plump, about 10 minutes.

3. Slice ham or chicken loaf into 8 slices.

4. Pan-fry in a hot cast-iron frying pan until browned on both sides.

5. Transfer to a platter or individual plates, drizzle with sauce, and serve hot.

helpful hint

Fresh cut flowers will last longer when 2 tablespoons of apple cider vinegar and 1 teaspoon of sugar are mixed into the water.

.99¢
.99¢
.99¢
.99¢
.99¢
ABOUT
$4.99

Red Flannel Hash 4 SERVINGS

"Hash" is a classic example of early American cooking, where various leftovers get transformed into something new, different, and delicious. It has been said that the "waste not, want not" mentality of early American settlers caused this dish to evolve. If you don't want to stand over the stove, you may follow the recipe up to mixing everything in the frying pan and instead turn the mixture into a greased 2-quart casserole and bake at 350°F for about 35 minutes.

1 cup Spice Box dried chopped onions (use fresh onions when available)

5 tablespoons Danish Creamery butter

1½ cups Clasico corned beef, diced

1½ cups Libby's whole white potatoes, diced

1½ cups Libby's beets, chopped

½ cup Knudsen sour cream

1 teaspoon Heinz Worcestershire sauce

Spice Supreme salt and pepper to taste

1. Soak dried onions in hot water for 5 to 10 minutes. Drain.

2. Sauté onions in 2 tablespoons butter for 1 to 2 minutes in a heavy-bottomed frying pan.

3. In a bowl, combine the beef, potatoes, beets, onions, sour cream, Worcestershire sauce, salt, and pepper.

4. Heat remaining butter in the frying pan; add the meat mixture and cook over low heat until heated through, stirring occasionally.

5. Continue to cook until browned and crusted underneath.

6. Place a serving platter over the pan and invert the hash, crusty side up. Serve hot or at room temperature.

helpful hint

Instead of pouring the beet juice down the drain, use it to replace that same amount of water when cooking rice. You'll have a "purpley" dish that will entice finicky children to the table.

.99¢
.99¢
.99¢
.99¢
.99¢
ABOUT
$4.99

Sloppy Joes 8 SANDWICHES

I became very excited when I discovered the meatballs one day. They opened the door to many recipes where ground beef is called for and no substitution would work. Since they come cooked, time is saved by simply heating. This is a great example of keeping an eye open for substitutions.

½ cup Spice Box dried chopped onions (use fresh onions when available)

2 tablespoons Danish Creamery butter

3 (14.5-ounce) cans Hereford meatballs and tomato sauce, drained

½ cup Forrelli mushroom pieces

4 tablespoons Bali's Best chili sauce

McCormick salt and pepper to taste

8 All American hamburger buns

1. Soak dried onions in hot water for 5 to 10 minutes. Drain.

2. In a frying pan, sauté onions in butter.

3. Crumble in meatballs and cook until heated through, about 3 to 4 minutes.

4. Add mushrooms, chili sauce, salt, and pepper. Blend and heat through.

5. Toast buns and fill with mixture. Serve hot.

helpful hint

For a more sophisticated version, replace the buns with homemade corn cups (see recipe in Toasts, Cups, and Stars at the end of the "Hors d'Oeuvres and Appetizers" section). Fill each cup with the mixture and serve as party hors d'oeuvres.

.99¢
.99¢
.99¢
.99¢
.99¢

ABOUT
$2.99

Pizza

There truly is no substitute for the taste of a crust made from scratch. The crusts can be frozen before cooking and stored for future use. They should be wrapped well and thoroughly thawed before cooking. The possibilities for toppings are endless: cheese, ham, chicken, pineapple, olives, artichoke hearts, and so on. An interesting version I like is just the sauce (recipe below) and sardines. So, be creative and enjoy!

CRUST 4 INDIVIDUAL PIZZA CRUSTS

1¼ cups lukewarm water

1 package Best Yet dry active yeast

3 cups Best Yet all-purpose flour

1½ teaspoons Spice Supreme salt

1 tablespoon Carapelli extra virgin olive oil

1. In a large mixing bowl, mix ½ cup lukewarm water (between 100° and 110°F) and yeast. Let stand for 10 minutes.

2. Add flour, salt, olive oil, and remaining water. Mix well and knead for ten minutes on a floured surface, adding flour as necessary to achieve a silky dough.

3. Place dough in an oiled bowl, cover with a cloth, and put in a warm place.

4. Wait until dough doubles in bulk (will take 1 hour or more). Punch down dough and let stand another 10 minutes.

5. Divide into four portions and roll into 10" circles. You can freeze it now or continue to prepare by brushing with olive oil and adding your favorite toppings.

6. Place on a baking sheet dusted with cornmeal or corn muffin mix and cook at 450°F for 10 to 15 minutes. Temperature can be reduced to 425° if crust seems to be getting too dark.

continued on facing page

.99¢
.99¢
.99¢
.99¢
.99¢
ABOUT
$1.99

Pizza CONTINUED

GREAT PIZZA SAUCE   ENOUGH FOR TWO PIZZA CRUSTS

1 (6-ounce) can Wegman's tomato paste

½ cup Hunt's crushed tomatoes

2 tablespoons El Pique menudo spice mix

1 teaspoon Gilroy Farms crushed garlic

Spice Supreme salt and pepper to taste

1. Combine all ingredients in a saucepan and heat for 1 minute.

2. Spread over crusts and follow with desired toppings.

helpful hint

Yeast dough will rise more quickly if the covered bowl is placed on a heating pad set at medium.

Baked Goods and Desserts

.99¢
.99¢
.99¢
.99¢
.99¢

ABOUT
$0.99

Pastry for Savory Pie Crust ONE CRUST FOR A
9" PIE PLATE (6–8 SERVINGS)

This crust will suffice for all your savory pies. It's simple and shortening can be substituted for the lard—but, once again, use either what you have or what you can find at the best store in the world! This is the base for the Hawaiian Ham Pie in "Main Courses."

1½ cups Best Yet all-purpose flour or 1 cup Manischewitz cake meal

½ teaspoon Spice Supreme salt

½ cup Rex lard

4 to 5 tablespoons cold water

1. Sift flour and salt together.

2. Cut in lard with a pastry cutter or a blending fork until mixture is the size of small peas.

3. Add water to one-fourth or one-fifth of the mixture at a time. Push a portion of the mixture to one side of the bowl and add 1 tablespoon of the cold water to it. Gently toss with fork.

4. Sprinkle another tablespoon of water over another portion of dry mixture; mix lightly and push to moistened side. Repeat this until all is moistened, using up the 4 to 5 tablespoons of water.

5. Form into a ball and proceed as directed in recipe.

helpful hint

Tossing ingredients with a fork, gently and quickly, will help prevent a tough pastry.

.99¢
.99¢
.99¢
.99¢
.99¢
ABOUT
$1.99

Hominy Cakes 8 TO 12 CAKES

Easier, crunchier, and less of a cliché than pancakes, these griddle treats are sure to please. In fact, I have lured some finicky munchkins to try these by reminding them that all good cowboys and cowgirls eat hominy cakes before working the ranch.

1 (1-pound) can Teasdale hominy

2 tablespoons Danish Creamery butter

1½ to 2+ cups Cinch pancake mix

1. Drain hominy, reserving the liquid. In a cast-iron pan over medium heat, melt the butter and lightly toast the hominy.

2. Transfer to a large mixing bowl and thoroughly mash the hominy with the reserved liquid. Add the pancake mix until a thick batter forms.

3. Drop large spoonfuls of the batter onto an oiled griddle and fry until browned and crispy.

4. Serve hot with pancake or fruit syrup.

helpful hint

For perfectly round griddle cakes, cut the bottom out of a clean recycled tuna can and grease the inside rim. Place the form on an oiled griddle and pour batter inside. Once the batter begins to firm up, remove the form, flip, and start another cake.

.99¢
.99¢
.99¢
.99¢
.99¢
ABOUT
$1.99

Naan 8 LOAVES

This leavened bread is a must to accompany Indian dishes. It is dense yet light, and the buttery outside makes the mouth water.

¾ cup lukewarm water

1 (¼-ounce) package Best Yet dried yeast

3 teaspoons Spreckels sugar

¼ cup plain Dannon yogurt, or substitute

1 Country egg, beaten

¼ cup Danish Creamery butter, melted, plus more for greasing

2 teaspoons McCormick salt

3½ cups Best Yet flour

2 tablespoons El Pique cumin seeds

1. Fill a small warm bowl with ¼ cup lukewarm water and sprinkle yeast on top. Leave for a few minutes to soften, then stir to dissolve.

2. Add 1 teaspoon sugar, stir, and leave in a warm place for 10 minutes, until it starts to froth. This is proofing the yeast. If it does not froth, start over with a new package of yeast.

3. Stir yogurt until smooth and mix with remaining sugar, remaining lukewarm water, egg, ¼ cup melted butter, and salt.

continued on facing page

helpful hint

To keep the naan warm, place a ceramic tile in the oven while cooking. When you are ready to serve, place the hot tile in the serving basket covered with a napkin with the naan on top.

Naan CONTINUED

4. Stir in the yeast mixture.

5. In another bowl, put 2 cups flour and make a well in the center. Pour the liquid in the well and beat until a smooth batter is formed.

6. Add remaining flour a bit at a time until stiff enough that you must start using your hands to knead.

7. Knead for 12 minutes, until dough is smooth and elastic. Add as little extra flour as possible.

8. Form into a ball and let rest.

9. Warm a large heat-proof bowl with boiling water for 3 minutes. Dry it well and grease it.

10. Put dough in bowl and then turn over so top is greased. Cover with a cloth and leave in a warm place until it has doubled in size and a finger leaves an impression.

11. Punch down and divide into eight balls. Let balls rest for 10 minutes.

12. Preheat oven to 450°F and place two ungreased baking sheets in the oven to heat.

13. Pat dough into circles about ¼ inch thick.

14. Pull one end out until the loaf resembles a teardrop the size of your hand, with the edges slightly thicker than the center. Repeat with remaining loaves.

15. Brush both sides of each loaf with melted butter and sprinkle with cumin seeds.

16. Place loaves on baking trays and cook until golden and puffy, about 10 minutes. You may brown under a broiler to achieve the desired color. Serve warm with a main dish or as a vehicle for your favorite spicy dips and spreads.

.99¢
.99¢
.99¢
.99¢
.99¢

ABOUT
$4.99

Raisin Bacon Muffins 12 MUFFINS

These sweet and savory muffins are a treat in the morning and go especially well with main course dishes such as Red Flannel Hash, Hopping John, and Frittata Italiana.

1 cup Champion raisins

3 cups Best Yet flour or 1 cup 7 ounces Manischewitz cake meal

6 teaspoons Hearth Club-Clabber Girl baking powder

¾ teaspoon Spice Supreme salt

2 tablespoons Spreckels sugar

2 tablespoons Rex lard

3 Foremost eggs

1 cup Springfresh milk

½ cup Branding Iron cooked, crisp, crumbled bacon

1. Preheat oven to 450°F.

2. Combine dry ingredients.

3. Work lard in with a pastry cutter or hands.

4. Combine eggs and milk and add to flour mixture. Add raisins and bacon and blend well.

5. Bake in a greased muffin pan until golden and toothpick comes out clean, about 25 minutes.

helpful hint

Say goodbye to "gunky" flour sifters. Instead of running them under water and being stuck with glue, store the sifter in a plastic bag. It won't get flour on your shelves and will be protected from dust.

.99¢
.99¢
.99¢
.99¢
.99¢
ABOUT
$2.99

Apricot Tartlettes 12 TARTLETTES

A good choice for a dessert buffet or as a sweet snack at a cocktail party. They go very well with cognac and are so darned cute! They can be quickly reheated or served at room temperature. Canned mandarin oranges can be used in place of the apricots for a tarter flavor.

1 (15-ounce) can Del Monte almond-flavored apricot halves

1¼ cups Honey Maid graham cracker crumbs

¼ cup Spreckels sugar

⅓ cup Imperial margarine, melted

¼ cup Patilla chocolate-hazelnut spread

¼ can Star Snacks toffee almonds, finely chopped

1. Preheat oven to 375°F.

2. Drain and dice apricots. Set aside.

3. Prepare graham crust by mixing crumbs, sugar, and margarine.

4. Mold into the cups of a mini muffin pan.

5. Bake for 5 to 6 minutes.

6. In such a small space, the crust will have a tendency to rise and close up the opening, so after removing from oven, press the crusts back down using the back of a metal teaspoon. Let cool.

7. Spoon a small amount of the chocolate-hazelnut spread into each cup, top with diced apricots, and sprinkle with a pinch of the chopped toffee almonds.

helpful hint

In a rush? To cut down on time and sweetness, pre-made biscuit or crescent roll dough can substitute for the graham shells. See One-Bite Ham and Cheese Pies in the "Hors d'Oeuvres and Appetizers" section for further instructions.

.99¢
.99¢
.99¢
.99¢
.99¢
ABOUT
$2.99

Flambéed Bananas Drizzled with Dulce de Leche 6 SERVINGS

This recipe is incredibly simple. Yet with its exotic taste and presentation your guests will feel they are at a five-star resort. After you feel comfortable with flambéing, feel free to let everyone see the moment you pour in the rum—you'll be the talk of the town. No one needs to know it only cost you 50¢ a serving!*

1 (14-ounce) can Magnolia sweetened condensed milk

3 tablespoons Imperial margarine or Danish Creamery butter

6 Conchita bananas

1 airline-size bottle (about ¼ cup) Christian Brothers white brandy or rum

continued on facing page

*Note: To flambé, you need to let the flame touch the alcohol. If you do not feel comfortable with this, don't worry—the taste is just as good without the drama.

helpful hint

Bananas tend to ripen faster than they can be consumed. A great way to avoid waste is to peel and freeze them. They can then be used at your leisure in smoothies and their frozen state makes adding ice unnecessary.

124

Flambéed Bananas
Drizzled with Dulce de Leche CONTINUED

1. First prepare the dulce de leche. I like doing it the old-fashioned way, which is exactly what the can tells you not to do, by putting the 14-ounce can *unopened* into a saucepan with enough water to cover entire can. However you make it, the dulce de leche can be prepared up to 3 days ahead if transferred to a container and refrigerated. Reheat by stovetop or microwave before serving.

2. For the unopened-can method, bring to a boil and then simmer very low for 3 hours. Be sure to add water so that the can is always covered, and keep the flame very low so that it doesn't explode! If you want to play it safe, pierce two holes in the top of the can and place it in a saucepan with enough water to come three-quarters of the way up the can.

3. Alternatively, you can pour the milk into a saucepan and boil on medium high heat for 1½ to 2 hours or until the liquid has thickened and turned a caramel color.

4. Melt butter or margarine in sauté pan.

5. Slice bananas lengthwise and brown on both sides, working gently to keep the bananas intact.

6. When pan is hot and bananas are well browned, remove from stove, pour rum into pan and return to the stove to flambé. Cook until liquid evaporates.

7. Arrange the banana halves on warmed plates and drizzle with dulce de leche. Serve immediately.

helpful hint
A waiter named Henri Carpentier is attributed to discovering flambé-ing. It was in Monte Carlo in 1895 when, as a waiter, he accidentally set fire to a of pan crepes. If only all of our culinary mishaps could end so sweetly.

.99¢
.99¢
.99¢
.99¢
.99¢
ABOUT
$3.99

Banana Bread Pudding with Dulce de Leche 6–8 SERVINGS

This is by far the most amazing, delicious, affordable, simple (yet extravagant) crowd-pleaser EVER! I came up with the idea of serving this when I knew that making the Flambéed Bananas for 20 would make me feel more like a short order cook than a hostess. This recipe doubles easily and it can be prepared hours in advance. Once cooked it can also be frozen and warmed up in a microwave. A perfect dessert for a big party, and so good for breakfast the next day.*

1 to 2 (14-ounce) cans Star sweetened condensed milk, for the dulce de leche

3 to 4 packed cups of cubed bread made from 1 loaf Premium white bread

2 very ripe Dole bananas

3 Country eggs

3 cups Springfresh milk or milk substitute (e.g., coconut milk)

⅓ cup Spreckels sugar

½ teaspoon McCormick salt

2 teaspoons Spice Classics vanilla extract

continued on facing page

*Note: You may omit the bananas or add 1½ cups of any chopped chocolate, if you desire.

helpful hint

Pint-size milk cartons are great for freezing blocks of ice for pitchers, allowing you to save your cubes for your guests.

126

Banana Bread Pudding with Dulce de Leche CONTINUED

1. There are two ways to prepare dulce de leche. The safer way is to pierce two holes in the top of the can of milk, place in a saucepan with enough water to come three-quarters of the way up the can, bring to a boil, and continue to boil on medium high heat for 1 to 2 hours for a runnier sauce or 3 to 4 hours for a more solid form.

2. The way I was brought up to do it is as follows: Fill a large saucepan and place the *unopened* can of sweetened condensed milk in the cool water, making sure the water comes up high enough to cover. Bring to a boil, then turn down heat and simmer about 3 hours. Add water occasionally so that the can is always covered, and make sure to keep the flame very low to avoid an explosion. Remove from heat and cool can thoroughly before opening.

3. In the meantime, spread the cubed bread on the bottom of a 9" × 13" baking dish and slice the bananas evenly, nestling them in the bread.

4. In a mixing bowl, combine eggs, milk, sugar, salt, and vanilla. Pour this custard over the bread

5. Bake in a preheated 350°F oven for about 30 minutes, until firm but not dry.

6. Serve either on individual plates, drizzling the dulce de leche on top, or set out so your guests can serve themselves with sauce on the side.

helpful hint
Attaching the inside of a banana skin to a nasty bruise will draw out the internal bleeding. (I used this recipe in 1990. The combination of my first night in Paris, the wine, and a flight of stairs had me sitting on a banana peel for a few days. It does work.)

.99¢
.99¢
.99¢
.99¢
.99¢

ABOUT
$3.99

Banana Date Bread 1 STANDARD LOAF OR 3 MINI LOAVES

This is a great solution to the economic stress of the holidays. Making, instead of buying, gifts is not the money-saver it used to be. Raw materials often cost more than the finished product! But these cute little loaves will only cost you about $1.15 each. And if you buy your gift wrap where you buy these groceries, you'll still stay under $2 a gift.

½ cup Dutch Farms Wisconsin Select margarine

1 cup Dole bananas, puréed (about 2 bananas)

2 Country eggs

1 cup Spreckels sugar

2 cups Best Yet all-purpose flour or 10 ounces Manischewitz cake meal

1 teaspoon Arm & Hammer baking soda

½ teaspoon Spice Supreme salt

1 cup Sweet Harvest chopped dates

1. Preheat oven to 450°F.

2. Mix all wet ingredients together and all the dry ingredients together, and then combine the two in a large bowl.

3. Pour into one standard, or three 6" x 3" x 2" mini loaf, greased and floured bread pans (which you can get at you-know-where).

4. Bake for 15 minutes then turn heat to 350°F and bake for another 45 minutes or until done (when a knife inserted in the center comes out clean).

helpful hint

Eat two ripe bananas to chase away the blues. They contain serotonin, a hormone which is boosted to treat depression.

.99¢
.99¢
.99¢
.99¢
.99¢
ABOUT
$1.99

Crazy Delicious 30-Minute Chocolate Cake 1 CAKE

Need I say more?

1 teaspoon Arm & Hammer baking soda

1½ cup Best Yet flour or Manischewitz cake meal

1 teaspoon Spice Classics vanilla extract

2 ounces (2 squares) Bakers unsweetened chocolate, shaved

1 cup cold water

½ teaspoon Spice Supreme salt

6 tablespoons Gold-N-Sweet vegetable oil

1 cup Spreckels sugar

1 tablespoon Citrovita vinegar

1. Preheat oven to 375°F.

2. Place all ingredients in an ungreased 9" × 9" × 2" pan. Stir with a fork until well blended.

3. Bake for 25 minutes. Cool in pan and frost as desired.

helpful hint

Using waxed dental floss to slice a cake in two for icing is much more reliable than using a knife. Simply cut a sufficient length, wrap it around the index fingers of both hands, and drag the "wire" through the cake.

.99¢
.99¢
.99¢
.99¢
.99¢
ABOUT
$3.99

Crème Caramel 8 SERVINGS

Classic and always appreciated, this dessert also has lots of variations. Instant coffee, tea, or extracts such as orange, lemon, or almond can be added to taste. If you wish, add one of these to the milk about an hour before preparation so that the flavors can infuse. To get flavors on the bold side, I use about 2 tablespoons of instant coffee or strongly brewed cold tea, or 2 teaspoons of extract.

1½ cups Spreckels sugar

3 tablespoons plus ⅓ cup water

11 Foremost eggs (6 whole eggs and 5 yolks)

1 quart Springfresh hot milk

2 teaspoons Spice Classics vanilla

Pinch salt

1. Caramelize the dish by bringing ¾ cup sugar and 3 tablespoons water to a simmer in a small heavy saucepan; slowly let it reach a boil.

2. Remove from heat and swirl pan until all sugar has been thoroughly dissolved.

3. Cover pan and boil mixture without stirring, until syrup is caramel brown.

continued on facing page

helpful hint

Filling large-size, washed milk or juice cartons with charcoal and lighting in a barbecue helps get the party started. The wax from the carton helps ignite the coals and keep them at a steady glow.

Crème Caramel CONTINUED

4. Pour half the caramel in baking dish; swirl it around to coat bottom and partway up the sides.

5. Add ⅓ cup water to remaining syrup in pan and simmer to dissolve. Set aside for extra sauce.

6. For the custard, preheat oven to 350°F.

7. Stir eggs, yolks, and remaining sugar in a bowl. Whip, but do not beat or make foamy.

8. Slowly pour in hot milk to dissolve sugar completely. Add vanilla and salt.

9. Pour mixture through a sieve into the caramelized dish. Skim any bubbles off surface.

10. Place dish in a baking pan. Pour boiling water into the pan so that it rises to two-thirds the height of the dish.

11. Place baking pan in lower third of oven. Regulate heat so that water does not return to a boil.

12. Bake for 45 minutes to 1¼ hours. Custard is done when a skewer plunged down an inch from the edge comes out clean.

13. Let settle for 30 minutes or more, and then run a thin sharp knife between custard and dish. Invert onto a platter and top with reserved sauce.

helpful hint
Sprinkling crushed egg-shells around the base of a plant may help ward off snails and slugs. They can serve a double service when also used as a marker for freshly planted seeds.

.99¢
.99¢
.99¢
.99¢
.99¢

ABOUT
$5.99*

Delicious Orange Cheesecake 10 SERVINGS

Since this needs time to set, it can be made up to a day in advance and will help save time on the day of your gathering. By pairing it with Wedding Day Chicken Supreme, you can get all your cooking done a day ahead and truly enjoy your company.

1¾ cups Honey Maid graham cracker crumbs

⅓ cup Imperial margarine, melted

1¼ cups Spreckels sugar, divided (103 packets, if you want to go that way)

24 ounces Philadelphia cream cheese, softened

2 teaspoons Spice Classics orange extract

3 Country eggs

1 cup Knudsen sour cream

1. Preheat oven to 350°F.

2. Combine crumbs, margarine, and ¼ cup of sugar. Press onto the bottom and up the sides of an 8" or 9" springform pan; set aside.

3. With an electric mixer on high speed, beat cream cheese, remaining cup of sugar, and extract until creamy.

4. Beat in eggs one at a time. Blend in sour cream.

5. Spread into prepared pan and bake for 60 to 70 minutes, until center is set.

6. Turn oven off, leaving door slightly ajar. After 1 hour, remove cake from oven and cool completely. Chill at least 4 hours. Remove from pan and serve.

*Or $9.99 depending on how the cream cheese is sized and priced.

helpful hint

Placing a shallow pan of water on the oven rack below the cheesecake will help keep the oven moist.

.99¢
.99¢
.99¢
.99¢
.99¢
ABOUT
$9.99

Strawberry Cheesecake 10 SERVINGS

The strawberry cream cheese was a one-time find for me; if you can't find it, you can mix a 15-ounce can of drained King's Pantry strawberries with plain cream cheese before adding it to the recipe.

1¾ cups Honey Maid graham cracker crumbs

⅓ cup Imperial margarine, melted

1¼ cups Spreckels sugar, divided (103 packets, if you want to go that way)

3 (8-ounce) containers Smith's Strawberry cream cheese

3 Country eggs

1 cup Knudsen dairy sour cream

1. Preheat oven to 350°F.

2. Combine crumbs, margarine, and ¼ cup of sugar. Press onto the bottom and up the sides of an 8" or 9" springform pan; set aside.

3. With an electric mixer on high speed, beat cream cheese and remaining cup of sugar until creamy.

4. Beat in eggs one at a time. Blend in sour cream.

5. Spread into prepared pan and bake for 60 to 70 minutes, until the center is set.

6. Turn oven off, leaving door slightly ajar. After 1 hour, remove cake from oven and cool completely. Chill at least 4 hours. Remove from pan and serve.

helpful hint

Cheesecakes can be kept for up to 2 months in the freezer. Securely wrap when already firm, after about 4 hours in the refrigerator.

.99¢
.99¢
.99¢
.99¢
.99¢
ABOUT
$4.99

Delicious Toffee Oatmeal Chocolate Chunk Cookies 3 DOZEN COOKIES

These are just what the name says . . . delicious!

1 cup Imperial margarine

1 cup Spreckels sugar

1 cup Lucky golden brown sugar

2 Country eggs

2 tablespoons Springfresh milk

1½ cups Best Yet all-purpose flour or 1 cup Manischewitz cake meal

½ teaspoon Spice Supreme salt

1 teaspoon Arm & Hammer baking soda

2 cups Good 'N Hearty quick rolled oats

1 (8-ounce) Zachary solid milk chocolate Easter bunny, chopped, or any milk chocolate bars available at the time

1 (4-ounce) can Star Snacks toffee almonds, chopped

1. Preheat oven to 375°F.

2. In a large mixing bowl, cream margarine and sugars, ½ cup at a time. Beat in eggs and milk.

3. Add flour, salt, and baking soda and beat well.

4. Add oats, chocolate chunks, and finally the almonds. Blend well.

5. Drop in rounded teaspoonfuls two inches apart onto an ungreased cookie sheet. Bake for 13 to 15 minutes. Remove and let cool.

helpful hint

For perfectly round cookies, pack the cookie dough inside a clean food can and refrigerate for at least 1 hour. Remove the bottom of the can with an opener and use the disc to push the dough out. Stop at your desired thickness and slice. Use the can as a guide.

.99¢
.99¢
.99¢
.99¢
.99¢
ABOUT
$1.99

Peanutty Peanut Butter Cookies 3 DOZEN COOKIES

Truly delectable (for those not allergic to peanuts, of course). The peanuts add a nice crunch, and using the tines of the fork to make an impression will really make an impression.

8 tablespoons Imperial margarine

½ cup Pica crunchy peanut butter

¾ cup Lucky golden brown sugar

2 tablespoons Family Choice pancake syrup

1 Country egg

1½ cups Best Yet all-purpose flour or 1 cup Manischewitz cake meal

¾ teaspoon Arm & Hammer baking soda

½ cup Regency honey roasted peanuts, coarsely chopped

1. Preheat oven to 375°F.

2. With an electric mixer, cream the margarine, peanut butter, and brown sugar. Add the syrup and egg.

3. In a separate bowl, blend flour, baking soda, and peanuts.

4. Slowly add flour mixture to the peanut butter mixture until incorporated.

5. Drop in rounded tablespoonfuls on cookie sheets and press down with tines of a fork. Bake for 8 to 10 minutes and let cool.

helpful hint

Dipping the spoon in some milk before scooping up cookie dough will help slide the dough off the spoon and onto the cookie sheet with ease.

.99¢
.99¢
.99¢
.99¢
.99¢
ABOUT
$3.99

Better for You Banana Bread 1 LOAF

This recipe has only egg whites and uses applesauce instead of butter, which makes it less rich and extremely moist. An inserted knife will not come out clean when done, so be careful not to overcook.

Pure and Simple cooking spray

½ cup Applesnax applesauce

1 cup Spreckels sugar

4 large ripe Conchita bananas, mashed

3 Country egg whites

1 teaspoon Spice Classics almond extract

2½ cups Best Yet flour or 12½ ounces Manischewitz cake meal

2 teaspoons Hearth Club-Clabber Girl baking powder

1 teaspoon Arm & Hammer baking soda

1 teaspoon Spice Supreme cinnamon

1 (4-ounce) can Star Snacks mixed nuts, chopped (optional)

1. Preheat oven to 350°F.

2. Spray a loaf pan with Pure and Simple cooking spray.

3. In a bowl, whisk the applesauce, sugar, mashed bananas, egg whites, and extract.

4. In a separate bowl, mix flour, baking powder, baking soda, and cinnamon.

5. Gently blend flour mixture into banana mixture and fold in nuts.

6. Pour into pan and cook 50 to 60 minutes.

helpful hint

The inside of a banana skin makes a great shoe polish. Rub it all over the shoe and then buff with a clean dry cloth. When you're done with that, bury the skin at the base of a rose bush. It will thank you with rich blooms.

.99¢
.99¢
.99¢
.99¢
.99¢
ABOUT
$4.99

Not "Too Regular" Regular Cake 2 CAKES

Don't worry! There are not enough prunes in a serving to have an effect on your body. This can be a great variation for a coffee cake or any morning treat.

1½ cups Spreckels sugar

1 cup Gold-N-Sweet vegetable oil

3 Country eggs

2 cups Best Yet flour or 10 ounces Manischewitz cake meal

1 teaspoon Arm & Hammer baking soda

1 teaspoon Spice Box nutmeg

1 teaspoon Spice Box cinnamon

1 teaspoon McCormick salt

1 cup 8th Continent soymilk, or milk substitute

1 teaspoon Spice Classics vanilla extract

1 cup Star Snacks nuts of choice, chopped (optional)

1 cup Sun Sweet ready-to-serve prunes, chopped (the kind that come in liquid)

1. Preheat oven to 300°F.

2. In a large bowl, blend sugar and oil. Add eggs and blend well.

3. In another bowl, sift together dry ingredients.

4. Add sifted dry ingredients and milk alternately to egg mixture.

5. Add vanilla, nuts, and prunes.

6. Bake in two greased 8" x 8" x 2" pans until done, about 30 to 45 minutes. Let cool and leave in pan until ready to serve.

helpful hint

Three hydrated prunes (either in juice or soaked in water for 2 hours) can improve memory and alleviate constipation. Eat some prunes—and then you should be able to remember to eat your prunes so you won't get constipated.

One-Bowl Brownies 24 BROWNIES

Of course, you could make brownies from a box mix, which seems to always be in stock. But making these from scratch is a great cozy pastime, especially when you have someone special to share them with. See the variations that follow to keep your brownie-making new and exciting.

4 ounces (4 squares) Bakers unsweetened baking chocolate

¾ cup Danish Creamery butter

2 cups Spreckels sugar

3 Country eggs

1 teaspoon Spice Classics vanilla extract

1 cup Best Yet flour or 5 ounces Manischewitz cake meal

1 cup Star Snacks cashew pieces, coarsely chopped

1. Preheat oven to 350°F, or 325°F if using a glass baking dish.

2. Line a 13" x 9" baking dish with foil, extending over the edges. Grease foil with margarine or spray.

3. Microwave chocolate and butter in a large bowl for about 2 minutes or until butter is melted. Stir until chocolate and butter are incorporated.

4. Add sugar and stir well. Mix in eggs and vanilla.

5. Stir in flour and nuts until well blended.

6. Spread into prepared pan. Bake 30 to 35 minutes or until toothpick in the middle comes out with crumbs.

7. Cool in pan. Lift out of pan and cut into squares.

continued on facing page

One-Bowl Brownies CONTINUED

CREAM CHEESE BROWNIES

One-Bowl Brownies, uncooked

8 ounces Philadelphia cream cheese

⅓ cup Spreckels sugar

1 Country egg

2 tablespoons Best Yet flour

1. Prepare brownie batter as directed. Spread in prepared pan.

2. In a bowl, beat cream cheese, sugar, egg, and flour.

3. Spoon mixture over brownie batter. Swirl with a knife to marbleize. Bake for 40 minutes.

continued on next page

helpful hint

To eliminate the mess when melting chocolate, line a sieve with heavy aluminum foil and melt the chocolate over boiling water. Then simply throw the foil away when finished. (This is a great substitute for a double boiler if you don't own one.)

One-Bowl Brownies CONTINUED

COCONUT ROCKY ROAD BROWNIES

One-Bowl Brownies, uncooked

2 cups diced coconut marshmallows (these are from the Marshmallow Cakes with the bottom cookie taken off), or 2 cups diced Stay Puff toasted coconut marshmallows

1 cup diced Nestle chocolate bar

1 cup Star Snacks chopped nuts

1. Prepare brownie batter as directed. Bake 30 minutes.

2. Immediately sprinkle with diced marshmallows, chocolate bar, and chopped nuts.

3. Bake another 3 minutes or until toppings melt together.

PEANUT BUTTER BROWNIES

One-Bowl Brownies, uncooked

$2/3$ cup Pica peanut butter

1. Prepare brownie batter as directed, reserving 1 tablespoon of the margarine, melted, and 2 tablespoons of the sugar. Spread brownie batter into prepared pan.

2. Mix reserved ingredients and peanut butter.

3. Spoon mixture over brownie batter. Swirl with knife to marbleize. Bake 30 to 35 minutes.

.99¢
.99¢
.99¢
.99¢
.99¢
ABOUT
$3.99

Peach Crisp 6 SERVINGS

This is a great recipe to whip up when on vacation. Commit it to memory—as long as you have a feel for the consistency of the topping, you don't have to worry about being perfectly accurate with the measurements.

4 cups Early Garden peaches, rinsed and drained

1 cup Best Yet flour or 5 ounces Manischewitz cake meal

¾ cups Spreckels sugar

½ teaspoon Spice Supreme cinnamon

1 stick Danish Creamery butter or Imperial margarine

1 cup Good 'N Hearty quick rolled oats

1. Preheat oven to 375°F.

2. Put peaches in a greased 9" × 13" Pyrex baking dish.

3. In a separate bowl, combine flour, sugar, and cinnamon.

4. With your fingers, blend in the butter until the mixture resembles coarse meal.

5. Add oats and sprinkle mixture on top of the peaches.

6. Bake until top is browned and crisp, about 25 minutes.

helpful hint

If you are more in the mood for a crumble instead of a crisp, add ⅓ cup brown sugar and omit the oats.

.99¢
.99¢
.99¢
.99¢
.99¢
ABOUT
$4.99

Pinot Noir Poached Pear Tart 8 SERVINGS

This tart is simple and perfect for a summer night's dessert. I used pinot noir but a merlot would work just fine. I made the first one with a pre-made Keebler piecrust, but for the sake of this recipe I have written it with a homemade crust, which makes a tasty difference.

½ box (1½ cups) Honey Maid graham cracker crumbs

2¼ cups Spreckels sugar

⅓ cup Imperial margarine

2 (15-ounce) cans Del Monte ginger-flavored pear halves

½ bottle Flynn pinot noir wine

1 cup Pompeian red wine vinegar

1½ tablespoons Encore dried rosemary

1 tablespoon Spice Supreme cinnamon

continued on facing page

helpful hint

To thoroughly infuse the flavor of the rosemary, the pears can be prepared a day in advance. If you're one for canning, the pears can be hot-packed and kept for up to one year.

142

Pinot Noir Poached Pear Tart CONTINUED

1. First make the crust by mixing together graham crumbs, ¼ cup sugar, and ⅓ cup of melted margarine.

2. Form into, and up the sides of, an 8" or 9" pie pan. (I like to use a springform pan but in this case it is not necessary.) Put aside.

3. Drain pears well.

4. In a saucepan large enough for pears and liquids, add wine, vinegar, remaining sugar, rosemary, and cinnamon.

5. Bring to a boil, stirring often, until thin syrup forms, about 5 minutes.

6. Add pears, reduce heat to medium, and gently boil, turning them in the syrup for about 5 minutes. Watch closely, since these are not fresh pears and you don't want them to get mushy.

7. Turn off heat and let pears sit in syrup until cooled.

8. Remove pears to a separate bowl with enough syrup to cover.

9. Return remaining syrup in saucepan to a boil and cook until it thickens to the consistency of a nice drizzling glaze. Remove from heat.

10. Cook crust at 375°F for 6 to 8 minutes and remove from oven, leaving oven on.

11. Carefully slice the pears lengthwise and layer into crust.

12. Return pie to oven just until pears are warm. Drizzle with the reduced syrup.

13. Serve alone, or à la mode when ice cream is available.

helpful hint
The name pinot noir is derived from the French words 'pine' and 'black' describing the dark, pine cone shaped grape clusters. It is a very versatile wine and goes wonderfully with all meats, creamy sauces and spicy seasonings.

.99¢
.99¢
.99¢
.99¢
.99¢
ABOUT
$1.99*

Warm Bundles 8 BUNDLES

So easy and so appreciated! You can really put anything inside. Get creative with both sweet and savory ideas. Ham, cheese, and even sautéed vegetables can transform this from a dessert to an hors d'oeuvres in a snap.

1 (8-ounce) container Pillsbury crescent roll dough

1 large Nestle milk chocolate bar or ½ cup of fruit, fruit filling, or fruit preserves of choice

1. Preheat oven to 350°F.

2. On a dusted surface, roll out the dough and separate along the perforations.

3. Place a square of the chocolate bar, or a tablespoon of fruit spread, or whatever filling(s) you've chosen on one-half of the dough sections.

4. Fold over, seal edges and bake for 8 to 11 minutes.

5. Serve immediately.

*Depending on filling you choose.

helpful hint

Place bowls with different fillings and the separated dough out on a work surface and you will instantly have a great activity and tasty snack for those kids who might otherwise be wreaking havoc in the house. This is especially great for a rainy day.

.99¢
.99¢
.99¢
.99¢
ABOUT .99¢
$5.99

Fruit Cocktail Cake 1 CAKE

It doesn't get easier than this. A colorful cake for morning, noon, or night.

1 large (30-ounce) can Dole tropical fruit salad, drained

2 ripe Dole bananas, mashed

2 cups Best Yet all-purpose flour or 10 ounces Manischewitz cake meal

1 teaspoon Arm & Hammer baking soda

1 teaspoon Hearth Club-Clabber Girl baking powder

1 teaspoon Spice Supreme salt

1½ cups Spreckels sugar

2 Country eggs, beaten

¾ cup Star Snacks cashew pieces

¾ cup Lucky brown sugar

1. Preheat oven to 325°F.

2. In a large bowl, mix all ingredients except nuts and brown sugar.

3. Turn into a 9" × 12" greased pan.

4. Top with nuts and brown sugar.

5. Bake for about 1 hour.

helpful hint

Running a cake knife under hot water before cutting into your fresh, moist cake will give you clean slices without all the crumbles.

.99¢
.99¢
.99¢
.99¢
ABOUT .99¢
$2.99

Pooh Bread 1 LARGE ROUND

If it is not devoured immediately out of the oven, this bread with its sweet essence makes wonderful toast and is really great for sandwiches.

1 (¼-ounce) package Best Yet dry yeast

¼ cup lukewarm water

1 teaspoon Sprekles sugar

1 Country egg

½ cup Pot-O-Gold syrup with honey

1 tablespoon Spice Box coriander

½ teaspoon Spice Supreme cinnamon

¼ teaspoon Spice Box cloves, ground

1½ teaspoons Spice Supreme salt

1 cup 8th Continent soymilk, warmed

6 tablespoons Dutch Farms Wisconsin margarine

4½ cups Best Yet flour

continued on facing page

helpful hint

Lightly oiling a measuring cup before filling it with honey or molasses will help the viscous liquid slide out easily.

Pooh Bread CONTINUED

1. Preheat oven to 300°F.

2. Proof the yeast by placing it in the water, which should be between 100° and 110°F. Add the sugar and let stand for 10 minutes.

3. In a separate bowl, combine the egg, honey, and spices and beat until fluffy.

4. Add the yeast mixture, warm milk, and margarine.

5. Add flour. Knead the dough with oiled hands until smooth. (This bread dough will be stickier than most, so oiling the hands will help—but do not add more flour.)

6. Place dough into an oiled bowl and cover with a cloth. Wait until it has doubled in size, about 1 hour.

7. Punch the dough down and knead again for 5 to 10 minutes.

8. Shape into a round loaf and let rise again until double, about 1½ hours.

9. Bake for 1 hour.

helpful hint
Though bears are notorious for raiding beehives, their honey dripped paws are really searching for the larva within. I don't know if A.A. Milne knew this, but suffice to say Winnie the Pooh's love for honey is a lot more palatable than the accurate alternative.

.99¢
.99¢
.99¢
.99¢
.99¢
ABOUT
$1.99

Fluffy Omelets 2 SERVINGS

This is a favorite in my family and a wonderful midnight treat after a night on the town. Because they are so fluffy they sit lightly in the tummy.

6 Country eggs, separated

2 tablespoons Danish Creamery butter

¼ cup Spreckels sugar

Deluxe apricot jam, or jam of choice

1. Whip egg whites with an electric mixer until stiff. Look for peaks to form.

2. In another bowl, beat egg yolks until lemon-colored.

3. Gently fold the yolks into the whites.

4. In a frying pan, melt 1 tablespoon of butter and add one-half of the egg mixture.

5. Cook until bottom is golden brown, fold over and cook a few minutes longer until golden on both sides and firm throughout.

6. Transfer to a warm plate and repeat steps with remaining egg mixture.

7. Sprinkle with sugar and serve with jam on the side.

helpful hint

A funnel is great for separating eggs. Place a funnel in a water glass and break eggs into it. The whites will slip through while the yolks remain to be placed into another container.

.99¢
.99¢
.99¢
.99¢
ABOUT .99¢
$4.99

Chocolate Coconut Crispy Treats 15 SQUARES

I am sure that everyone, young or old, is familiar with the plain name-brand version of these. Try this variation—it is sinfully delicious.

4 ounces Danish Creamery butter

4 boxes coconut Marshmallow Cakes, 40 Stay Puff toasted coconut marshmallows, or 5½ cups mini marshmallows

6 cups Breakfast Choice coco crispies

1. Melt butter in a saucepan.

2. Remove bottom wafer from each marshmallow cake.

3. Add marshmallows to the butter and stir until melted.

4. Add coco crispies and mix well.

5. Press into a wax-paper-lined square pan.

6. Press another piece of wax paper over top and press again to achieve an even shape.

7. Let cool at least 30 minutes. Cut into squares and serve.

helpful hint

If you cannot find marshmallows, substitute 1 cup sugar, 1 cup corn syrup (light or dark), 1 teaspoon vanilla, and 1 cup peanut butter. Corn syrup will make the treats chewier than their softer marshmallow cousins.

.99¢
.99¢
.99¢
.99¢
.99¢
ABOUT
$1.99

Violet's Morning Cake 8 SERVINGS

My grandfather ate a piece of this every morning for as long as I remember. Violet, my grandmother, made it from scratch, of course, but I have recreated it within the guidelines of this book. The apricot jam is the special touch. Since this is made with a mix, where there is no control over the amount of sugar, the tartness of the apricot jam balances out the sweetness of the cake.

1 (18.25-ounce) box Duncan Hines Moist Deluxe butter recipe cake mix

3 Country eggs

½ cup (1 stick) Imperial margarine

⅔ cup water

1 tablespoon Spice Classics orange extract

1 cup Deluxe apricot jam

1. Prepare two 9" cakes according to instructions on box, adding the orange extract to the batter.

2. Let cool. Spread the apricot jam on the top of one cake and put the other cake on top of it.

3. Wrap tightly and refrigerate. Serve with coffee or tea.

helpful hint

Most people just grease baking pans and more times than not find the cake still sticks. Greasing and flouring will help considerably. Using a large powder puff to dust the pans will keep your kitchen tidy.

.99¢
.99¢
.99¢
.99¢
.99¢
ABOUT
$0

Recipe for Happiness INFINITE SERVINGS

This literally fell into my lap, out of a vintage cookbook I had bought at a flea market. Unfortunately, it was not signed, so I am unable to give credit to the writer. I trust that you will find this as charming as I did on that day.

2 cups Good Thoughts

1 cup Kind Deeds

1 cup Consideration for Others

3 cups Forgiveness

2 cups Well-Beaten Faults

1. Mix the above thoroughly.

2. Add tears of sorrow, sympathy, and flavor with little gifts of love.

3. Fold in 4 cups of hope and faith to lighten and raise texture to great heights of character.

4. Pour this into your daily life, bake with the heat of your heart, and serve with a smile.

Equivalents and Substitutions

Elementary school, and the measurements I was taught then, are vague memories to me. Liquid and dry differences, let alone the occasional metric recipe that falls in my lap, can make a relaxing day of cooking feel more like taking the SAT. Some people are very particular about using different measuring devices for liquid and dry ingredients. Weight and volume are, of course, two very different things. Most recipes are planned by volume, so 1 cup of milk is the same measurement as 1 cup of, say, flour.

The recipes in this book have all been created using a standard measuring cup (with ounce and cup markings) and a tablespoon/teaspoon collection. Sometimes I might be cooking so many things that I find my measuring devices not ready for the next use. Some of the equivalents below are useful when your measuring cup is full of flour and you have to use a tablespoon to measure out ½ cup of stock. I am therefore always thankful to have the guides provided in some of my cookbooks and felt it my duty to pass this information on to you. This also gave me the perfect excuse to gather all the tables and charts I have acquired and put all the pertinent information in one place. As for substitutions, well, needless to say, this book could not have been written without them. There is nothing that bugs me more than being in the middle of culinary expression and having to stop everything to run to the store for that missing ingredient. Bending as opposed to breaking is a much easier existence, but it does take some practice. Learning how to work with what you've got is a good place to start. Through the years I have learned all sorts of ways to get around brick walls in the kitchen and in life.

In the following pages you will find many ways to use what is available in place of what is not. I have included alternatives in some of the recipes, mainly to remind the reader of this section. In addition to being of help with the recipes in this book, I hope that these will also help you at times with your other culinary ventures. Remember, with an open and creative mind, you can overcome any obstacle.

General Temperatures

	FAHRENHEIT	CENTIGRADE
Freezer	0°	–17°
Coldest Part of Freezer (depends on settings)	about –10°	–23°
Water Freezes	–32°	0°
Water Boils	212°	100°
Deep Fat (for frying)	375°–400°	190°–204°
Hot Oven	450°	232°
Broil	550°	288°

Oven Temperatures and Settings

	FAHRENHEIT	CENTIGRADE	GAS MARK
Cool	225°	110°	¼
Very Slow	275°	140°	1
Slow	325°	170°	3
Moderate	350°	180°	4
Moderately Hot	400°	200°	6
Fairly Hot	425°	220°	7
Hot	450°	230°	8
Very Hot	475°	240°	9
Extremely Hot (just before broil)	500°	250°	10

Chile Pepper Temperatures (based on the Scoville Heat guide)

Wilbur Scoville was a pharmacologist who in 1912 created a way of measuring heat in a pepper by calculating the amount of water necessary to neutralize the capsaicin's (the active component of chili peppers) pungency. A bell pepper rates 0, a jalapeño 3,500 to 4,500, and the hottest of hot, the Naga Jolokia, comes in at 1,040,000. Occuring in Northeastern India, it comes in second only to standard U.S. grade pepper spray. Included are the Scoville ratings and a 1 to 10 equivalent to make it a little easier.

ANAHEIM: 1,000–1,400/2–3. A long green or red chile. Good for roasting and stuffing. Reds tend to be sweeter.

ANCHO: 1,000/4. A dried poblano. Used in moles and other sauces. The seeds are what makes this a 4. Remove them and the heat will go down.

BELL AND PIMIENTO: 0/0. The average no-heat pepper found at the grocery store. Greens have a more bitter taste, while the reds are sweeter. Roasting the reds creates the pimiento. These are very tasty on sandwiches such as grilled eggplant and goat cheese. Pimientos dried and ground become paprika.

CAYENNE: 35,000/8–9. A perfect hue of red, and cousin to the tabasco. Also known as de Arbol or the ginnie pepper. Used in Louisiana hot sauces and ground into a dry pepper.

CHILTECPIN: 70,000–75,000/8–9. Orange or red, this chile is used dried and fresh to season cooked dishes such as soups and stews. Gives a blast of heat that fades fast.

CHIPOTLE: 10,000/5. A smoked jalapeño. They have a nutty, fruity, woody taste that adds a great edge to many sauces.

HABANERO: 200,000–300,000/10. Ranges from green to yellow to orange to red. The hottest of the hot without a lasting burn. It has a fruity quality and is great in sauces, with fish, and with fruit.

JALAPEÑO: 3,500–4,500/5–6. Green to red when ripe. The most popular pepper in graphic design. It has a good balance of flavor and heat, so it is very versatile and a nice addition to any dish.

NAGA JOLOKIA: 855,000–1,41,427/HOT! Orange or red and similar in appearance to the habanero, but with a rough dented skin. The hottest chile in the world. Use with caution!

NEW MEXICAN: 1,000/3. Basically the Anaheim. Used fresh and dried. Versatile and great in tamales.

PASILLA: 2,500/4. Chile Negro. Mild and great for mole sauces.

PEQUIN: 75,000/4. Small and bright red. Used dried and fresh, it is hot and citrusy.

POBLANO: 2,500/3. Dark green to dark red. Red is sweeter, and when dried is known as the ancho, which rates at 1,000/2. A roasted poblano is perfect for a smoky addition.

SCOTCH BONNET: 300,000/10. The Jamaican version of the habanero. Bright/hot and fruity.

SERRANO: 7,000–25,000/7. As you can see, these little devils are unpredictable. Great for homemade hot sauces and sauces to accompany a meal. Be careful and test them first.

TABASCO: 30,000–50,000/9. Last but not least. The sauce known by the same name is my favorite condiment, but a much lower rating of 2,500-5,000. This pepper has a great heat.

EQUIVALENTS

Measurements

1 teaspoon = 60 drops = ⅓ tablespoon = 5 milliliters

2 teaspoons = ¼ fluid ounce = 7 milliliters

1 tablespoon = 3 teaspoons = ½ fluid ounce = 15 milliliters

2 tablespoons = 1 fluid ounce = 28 milliliters

4 tablespoons = ¼ cup = 2 fluid ounces = 56 milliliters

5⅓ tablespoons = ⅓ cup = 62 milliliters

8 tablespoons = ½ cup = 4 fluid ounces = 1 teacup = ¼ pint = 110 milliliters

¾ cup = 6 fluid ounces = 170 milliliters

16 tablespoons = 1 cup = ½ pint = 8 fluid ounces = 225 milliliters

⅜ cup = ¼ cup+2 tablespoons

⅝ cup = ½ cup+2 tablespoons

⅞ cup = ¾ cup+2 tablespoons

1 cup = ½ pint = 8 ounces = 225 milliliters

2 cups = 1 pint = 16 ounces = 450 milliliters

2¼ cups = 18 fluid ounces = 500 milliliters = ½ liter

3 cups = 1½ pints =24 fluid ounces = 675 milliliters

4 cups = 2 pints = 1 quart = 32 fluid ounces = 900 milliliters

4½ cups = 36 fluid ounces = 1,000 milliliters = 1 liter

6 cups = 3 pints = 1,350 milliliters

1 gallon = 4 quarts = 128 fluid ounces = 3 liters = 600 milliliters

EQUIVALENTS

Weight (Dry) Measures

1 ounce = 28 grams

2 ounces = 56 grams

3½ ounces = 100 grams

4 ounces = ¼ pound = 112 grams

8 ounces = ½ pound = 225 grams

9 ounces = 250 grams = ¼ kilo

12 ounces = ¾ pound = 340 grams

16 ounces = 1 pound = 450 grams

20 ounces = 1¼ pounds = 560 grams

24 ounces = 1½ pounds = 675 grams

36 ounces = 2¼ pounds = 1 kilo

EQUIVALENTS

Can Equivalents

6 ounce can = 6 ounces = ¾ cup

8 ounce can = 8 ounces = 1 cup

No. 1 can = 11 ounces = 1⅓ cup

12 ounce can = 12 ounces = 1½ cups

No. 303 can = 16 ounces = 2 cups

No. 2 can = 20 ounces = 2½ cups

No. 2½ can = 28 ounces = 3½ cups

EQUIVALENTS

Specific Equivalents

ALMONDS W/SHELLS: 1 pound = 1¾ cups meat

BACON: ½ pound = 9–10 slices

BACON, RENDERED: 1 pound = 1½ cups grease

BANANAS: 3–4 medium = 1 pound = 2 cups mashed

BEANS, NAVY: 1 pound = 2⅓ cups = 6 cups cooked

BREAD: 1 slice, dried = ⅓ cup crumbs

BUTTER: 1 pound = 2 cups = 4 sticks

CABBAGE: ½ pound, minced = 3 cups, packed

CHEESE: 1 pound = 4 cups grated

CHEESE, COTTAGE: 1 pound = 2 cups

CHEESE, CREAM: 3 ounces = 6 tablespoons

CHOCOLATE, UNSWEETENED: ½ pound = 8 1-ounce squares

COCONUT: 1 pound = 5 cups shredded

COCONUT, DRIED: 1 tablespoon dried = 1½ tablespoons fresh

COFFEE: 1 pound = 80 tablespoons = 40 cups

CORN MEAL: 1 cup uncooked = 4 cups cooked

EGG, WHITES: 11–12 = 1 cup

EGG, YOLKS: 12–14 = 1 cup

FLOUR, ALL-PURPOSE: 1 pound = 4 cups, sifted

FLOUR, CAKE: 1 pound = 5 cups, sifted

continued...

GRAHAM CRACKERS: 11 crushed = 1 cup crumbs

LEMON: 1 medium = 3 tablespoons juice

MACARONI: 1 cup uncooked = 2 cups cooked

MARSHMALLOWS: ½ pound = 16 whole (normal-size, not miniature);
1 normal-size marshmallow = 13 miniature marshmallows;
40 miniature marshmallows = ½ cup

MEAT: 1 pound = 2 cups ground

ORANGE: 1 medium = ⅓ cup juice

PEAS, COOKED: 1 pound = 5½ cups

PEAS, SPLIT: 1 pound = 2 cups dried = 5 cups cooked

PECANS W/SHELLS: 1 pound = 2½ cups meat

SUGAR, BROWN: 1 pound = 2¼ cups, firmly packed

SUGAR, CONFECTIONERS': 1 pound = 3½ cups, sifted

SUGAR, GRANULATED: 1 pound = 2 cups

WALNUTS W/SHELLS: 1 pound = 1⅔ cups, chopped

WHIPPING CREAM: ½ pint = 2 cups whipped

SUBSTITUTIONS

It's always best to follow the recipe as it is written, but in a jam, substitutions can save the day.

BAKING POWDER: 1 teaspoon = 1/3 teaspoon baking soda + 1/2 teaspoon cream of tartar, or 1/4 teaspoon baking soda + 1/2 cup yogurt.

BREAD CRUMBS: 1 cup = 1 cup matzo meal.

BUTTER: Take into consideration what the recipe is before making a substitution. For instance, you probably don't want to substitute bacon fat if making a dessert recipe. 1 cup = 1 cup margarine, or 4/5 cup clarified bacon fat, or 3/4 cup clarified chicken fat, or 7/8 cup corn oil, or 7/8 cup lard, or 7/8 cup vegetable shortening, or 1 cup various nut butters. Applesauce (for baking only) can replace up to 3/4 of the butter called for.

BUTTERMILK: 1 cup = 1 cup yogurt.

CHOCOLATE, SWEETENED: 1 unsweetened square + 4 teaspoons sugar = 1 2/3 ounces semi-sweet chocolate.

CHOCOLATE, UNSWEETENED: 1 square = 3 tablespoons cocoa + 1 tablespoon fat.

COCONUT CREAM: 1 cup = 1 cup cream.

COCONUT MILK: 1 cup = 1 cup milk.

CRACKER CRUMBS: 3/4 cup = 1 cup bread crumbs.

CREAM: 1 cup = 1/3 cup butter + 3/4 milk.

CREAM, SOUR: 3 tablespoons butter + 7/8 cup soured milk. (To sour milk: add 1 tablespoon lemon juice or vinegar to 1 cup minus 1 tablespoon lukewarm milk. Let stand 5 minutes.)

continued...

EGGS: 1 egg = ¼ cup soft tofu (mix in a food processor to ensure a smooth texture), or ½ banana, or 3 tablespoons applesauce (the last two for desserts and baked goods).

FLOUR, ALL-PURPOSE: 1 cup sifted = ⅝ cup cake meal, or 1 cup + 2 tablespoons cake flour, or 1 cup pancake mix (omit or lessen baking soda and powder in recipe when using pancake mix—compare recipe to pancake mix ratio of these).

FLOUR, CAKE: 1 cup sifted = 1 cup less 2 tablespoons all-purpose flour.

FLOUR, FOR THICKENING: 1 tablespoon = 1½ teaspoons cornstarch, or 2 teaspoons quick-cooking tapioca.

FLOUR, WHITE: 1 cup = 1 cup corn meal, or 1½ cups ground rolled oats (this will cook more slowly).

GARLIC: 1 clove = ⅛ teaspoon powdered.

GINGER: 1 tablespoon raw = 1 tablespoon candied (washed of sugar) = ⅛ teaspoon powdered.

HERBS: 1 tablespoon fresh = ⅓ to ½ teaspoon dried.

HONEY: ¾ cup = 1 cup white sugar (more or less to taste—remember that honey is about twice as sweet as sugar).

HORSERADISH: 1 tablespoon fresh = 2 tablespoon bottled = 2 tablespoons dried.

LEMON: 1 teaspoon juice = ½ teaspoon vinegar.

SUBSTITUTIONS

continued...

MILK: 1 cup = ½ cup evaporated milk + ½ cup water = 1 cup coconut milk = 1 cup soy milk = 1 cup skim + 3 tablespoons cream (see cream) = 4 parts dried to 1 part water (see package for whole or skim).

MUSHROOMS: 1 pound fresh = 6 ounces canned.

ONIONS: ½ cup fresh chopped = ½ cup dried chopped, reconstituted.

SALT: Soy sauce to taste.

SUGAR, FOR BAKING: 1 cup = 1 cup molasses + ¼ to ½ teaspoon baking soda (omit baking powder from recipe and reduce other liquids ¼ cup for every ¼ cup molasses) = ½ cup maple syrup + ¼ cup corn syrup mixed then minus 2 tablespoons = 1 cup honey. (Honey is about twice as sweet as sugar; you must add to taste. One rule to follow is: breads and rolls can use same amount of honey for sugar; cakes and cookies use ⅞ cup for every cup of sugar, with liquid in recipe reduced by 3 tablespoons for each cup of honey. Warm honey and mix with other wet ingredients to ensure proper distribution. Lighter honey will not corrupt the taste as much as a dark may.)

SUGAR, BROWN, PACKED: 1 cup = 1 cup white sugar

SUGAR, CONFECTIONERS': 1¾ cups = 1 cup white sugar

SUGAR, MAPLE: ½ cup = 1 cup maple syrup

YOGURT: 1 cup = 1 cup buttermilk = 1 cup milk + 1 teaspoon lemon juice

Glossary of Cooking Terms

GLOSSARY OF COOKING TERMS

BAKE: to cook food with the indirect dry heat of an oven. Covering food while baking it preserves moistness; leaving food uncovered results in a drier or crisper surface.

BEAT: to stir briskly with a spoon, with a whisk, with a hand egg beater, or with an electric mixer.

BLEND: to mix two or more ingredients until they make a uniform mixture.

BOIL: to cook a liquid at a temperature at which bubbles rise and break on the surface.

BRING TO A BOIL: Heat just until bubbling begins. In a full or rolling boil, the bubbles are larger and form quickly and continuously.

BROIL: to cook food directly under a direct source of intense heat or flame, producing a browned or crisp exterior and a less well done interior.

CHOP: to cut into small, irregular pieces with a knife or food processor.

COAT: to cover a food completely with an outer "coating" of another food or ingredient.

COARSELY CHOP: to cut food in to small pieces about $^3/_{16}$ in. (½ cm).

CREAM: to beat a fat until it is light and fluffy, often in combination with sugar or other ingredients.

CRUMBLE: to break food into smaller pieces usually by hand..

CUBE: to cut food into squares about ½ inch on the sides.

GLOSSARY OF COOKING TERMS

CUT IN: to combine a solid fat with dry ingredients, until the fat is in very small pieces about the size of small peas, by using a pastry blender or a fork. Compare with "cream."

DEEP-FRY: to cook food in hot, liquefied fat (usually kept at 350 to 375 degrees) deep enough to cover and surround the food completely.

DICE: to cut into reasonably uniform pieces of about ¼ inch.

DREDGE: to lightly coat food that is going to be fried with flour, breadcrumbs, or cornmeal. Dredged foods need to be cooked immediately, while breaded foods (dredged in flour, dipped in egg, then dredged again in breading) can be prepared in advance.

DRIZZLE: to pour a liquid topping in thin, irregular lines over a food.

DUST: to sprinkle a dry ingredient lightly and fairly evenly over a food.

FOLD: to combine ingredients gently, using a spatula or spoon to lift ingredients from the bottom of the bowl and "fold" them over the top.

FRY: to cook in hot fat or oil, producing a crisp exterior.

GREASE: to coat the surface of a pan with shortening or cooking spray to prevent foods from sticking while they bake. To "grease and flour" is to dust the pan lightly with flour after applying the shortening.

GRILL: to cook foods directly above a source of intense heat or flame. Foods can be pan-grilled on a stovetop by using a specially designed pan with raised grill ridges.

GLOSSARY OF COOKING TERMS

KNEAD: to work dough by continuous folding over and pressing down until it is smooth and elastic. Dough can also be kneaded with electric mixer attachments called dough hooks.

MARINATE: to let food stand in a special liquid to flavor it or tenderize it. The liquid is called a marinade.

MELT: to bring an ingredient to a liquid state by adding heat.

MINCE: to chop food into very small bits.

PAN-FRY: to fry with little or no added fat, using only the fat that accumulates during cooking.

PARBOIL: to cook fruits, vegetables, or nuts very briefly in boiling water or steam, usually to preserve the color or nutritional value or to remove the skin.

POACH: to cook in a simmering (not boiling) liquid.

PURÉE: to make into a thick liquid, usually by using a blender or food processor.

REDUCE: to boil a liquid until some of it evaporates, thus concentrating the flavor.

SAUTÉ: to cook in a small amount of fat over high heat.

SHRED: to cut in narrow, thin strips, usually by using a kitchen shredder. A knife can be used to shred lettuce or cabbage.

SIFT: to process dry ingredients through a kitchen sifter. Sifting adds air to dry ingredients that have been compressed in storage and also removes any lumps.

GLOSSARY OF COOKING TERMS

SIMMER: to keep a liquid just below the boiling point; a few bubbles will rise and break on the surface.

SKIM: to remove fat or foam that has accumulated on the surface of a liquid, usually using a spoon.

SLICE: to cut into flat pieces that are usually thin and even.

STEAM: to cook food above (not in) boiling or simmering water.

STIR: to mix ingredients at a moderate pace to combine them.

STIR-FRY: to cook small pieces of food in a hot wok or skillet, using a small amount of fat and a constant stirring motion.

STRAIN: to separate any solids from a liquid usually accomplished with a sieve or cheesecloth.

TOSS: to mix ingredients by gently lifting them from the bottom of the bowl and allowing them to tumble, usually using two forks or other utensils.

WHIP: to beat rapidly with a wire whisk, hand beater, or electric mixer. Whipping increases volume because it adds air to the ingredient(s).

Create Your Own Recipes

My 99¢ Only Stores Recipe

RECIPE NAME ....

SERVINGS ....

INGREDIENTS ....

....

....

....

....

....

....

....

....

DIRECTIONS ....

....

....

....

....

....

....

....

....

....

NOTES ....

....

....

My 99¢ Only Stores Recipe

RECIPE NAME ....

SERVINGS ....

INGREDIENTS ....

....

....

....

....

....

....

....

....

DIRECTIONS ....

....

....

....

....

....

....

....

NOTES ....

....

....

My 99¢ Only Stores Recipe

RECIPE NAME ....

SERVINGS ....

INGREDIENTS ....

....

....

....

....

....

....

....

....

DIRECTIONS ....

....

....

....

....

....

....

....

....

NOTES ....

....

....

My 99¢ Only Stores Recipe

RECIPE NAME ....

SERVINGS ....

INGREDIENTS ....

....

....

....

....

....

....

....

....

DIRECTIONS ....

....

....

....

....

....

....

....

NOTES ....

....

....

My 99¢ Only Stores Recipe

RECIPE NAME ....

SERVINGS ....

INGREDIENTS ....

....

....

....

....

....

....

....

....

DIRECTIONS ....

....

....

....

....

....

....

NOTES ....

....

....

My 99¢ Only Stores Recipe

RECIPE NAME ....

SERVINGS ....

INGREDIENTS ....

....

....

....

....

....

....

....

....

DIRECTIONS ....

....

....

....

....

....

....

....

NOTES ....

....

....

My 99¢ Only Stores Recipe

RECIPE NAME ....

SERVINGS ....

INGREDIENTS ....

....

....

....

....

....

....

....

....

DIRECTIONS ....

....

....

....

....

....

....

NOTES ....

....

....

My 99¢ Only Stores Recipe

RECIPE NAME ....

SERVINGS ....

INGREDIENTS ....

....

....

....

....

....

....

....

....

....

DIRECTIONS ....

....

....

....

....

....

....

....

....

NOTES ....

....

....

My 99¢ Only Stores Recipe

RECIPE NAME ....

SERVINGS ....

INGREDIENTS ....

....

....

....

....

....

....

....

....

....

DIRECTIONS ....

....

....

....

....

....

....

....

....

....

NOTES ....

....

....

My 99¢ Only Stores Recipe

RECIPE NAME ....

SERVINGS ....

INGREDIENTS ....

....

....

....

....

....

....

....

....

DIRECTIONS ....

....

....

....

....

....

....

....

....

NOTES ....

....

....

My 99¢ Only Stores Recipe

RECIPE NAME ....

SERVINGS ....

INGREDIENTS ....

....

....

....

....

....

....

....

....

DIRECTIONS ....

....

....

....

....

....

....

....

NOTES ....

....

....

My 99¢ Only Stores Recipe

RECIPE NAME ....

SERVINGS ....

INGREDIENTS ....

....

....

....

....

....

....

....

....

DIRECTIONS ....

....

....

....

....

....

....

....

NOTES ....

....

....

My 99¢ Only Stores Recipe

RECIPE NAME

....

SERVINGS

....

INGREDIENTS

....

....

....

....

....

....

....

....

....

....

DIRECTIONS

....

....

....

....

....

....

....

....

....

NOTES

....

....

....

My 99¢ Only Stores Recipe

RECIPE NAME ....

SERVINGS ....

INGREDIENTS ....

....

....

....

....

....

....

....

....

....

....

DIRECTIONS ....

....

....

....

....

....

....

....

....

....

NOTES ....

....

....

My 99¢ Only Stores Recipe

RECIPE NAME
....

SERVINGS
....

INGREDIENTS
....

....

....

....

....

....

....

....

....

DIRECTIONS
....

....

....

....

....

....

....

....

NOTES
....

....

....

My 99¢ Only Stores Recipe

RECIPE NAME ....

SERVINGS ....

INGREDIENTS ....

....

....

....

....

....

....

....

....

DIRECTIONS ....

....

....

....

....

....

....

....

NOTES ....

....

....

Index

Disney
fairies

Fairy Glow

Phidal

Introducing the Fairies

Get to know each of the fairies by placing your stickers above their names.

Silvermist

Water Fairy

Tinker Bell

Tinker Fairy

Iridessa

Light Fairy

Rosetta

Garden Fairy

Vidia

Fast-flying Fairy

Fawn

Animal Fairy

Natural Beauty

Use your stickers to match each fairy with the natural material of their clothing.

Leaves

Sunflowers

Lilies

Moss

Roses

Feathers

Violets

Baby's Breath

Snowflakes

Tiger Lilies

Leaves

Acorns

Pixie Dust Tree

Fairies need pixie dust to be able to fly. Decorate the scene below using your stickers.

Talented Fairies

Fairies are born with special talents. Help match each fairy to their unique talent.

Animal Fairy

Light Fairy

Tinker Fairy

Garden Fairy

Fast-flying Fairy

The Four Seasons

Can you name all the seasons? Match each minister to their season using your stickers.

Minister
of Spring

Minister
of Summer

Minister
of Autumn

Minister
of Winter

Who's who?

Let's take a closer look! Use the close-up clues to help identify each fairy.

Stunning Sunflowers

Make the stunning sunflower meadow below identical to the one above it.

Pixie Dust

Phidal

Special Spots

Fairies have special places they like to visit. Place each fairy in their favorite setting.

Memorable Moments

Relive these memorable moments by matching each scene with the right sticker.

Fall Fanfare

The fairies are getting ready to celebrate the rare blue moon. Decorate the scene below.

Minister Match

Match each minister with the correct seasonal object using your stickers.

Spring or Fall?

The fairies know how to dress for any occasion! Place the fairies in the right season.

Fairy Patterns

Fairies love to play games! Complete these playful patterns below using your stickers.

Fairy Friends

Tink enjoys spending time with her fairy friends! Recreate the scene below.

Fairy Friendship

Phidal

Sneak Peek

Let's take a closer peek to identify each of these fairy friends.

High Flyers

The fairies love to fly high above the clouds! Use your stickers to decorate the scene.

3

4 5

6 11

Animal Families

Help Fawn sort her bird and insect friends into two groups using your stickers.

Birds

Insects

Fairy Opposites

Use your stickers to help Silvermist find each of these fairy opposites.

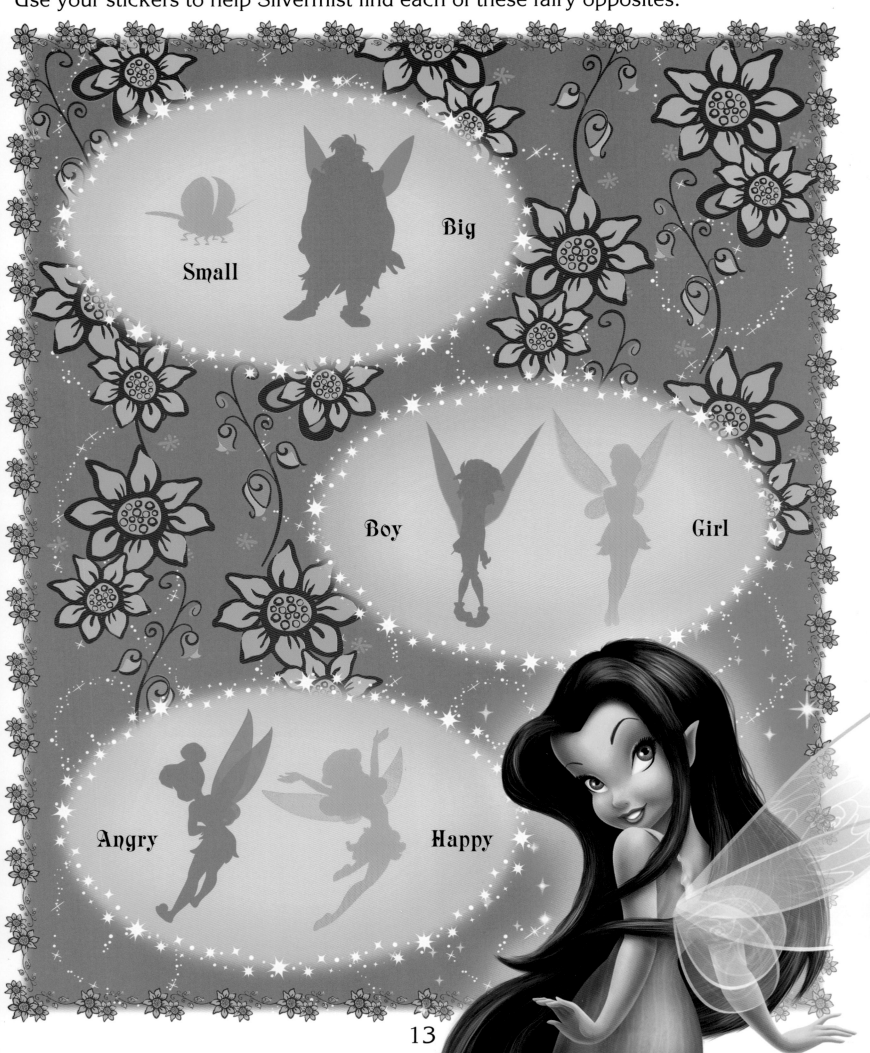

Small

Big

Boy

Girl

Angry

Happy

13

Life Lessons

Tink has learned a lot from her fairy friends! Complete the scenes using your stickers.

Caring Fairies

Tink's friends are there to help her back up after a tumble! Recreate the scene below.

Counting with Tinker Bell

Phidal

Count from 1 to 10

Count the objects in each circle. Use your stickers to find the right answer.

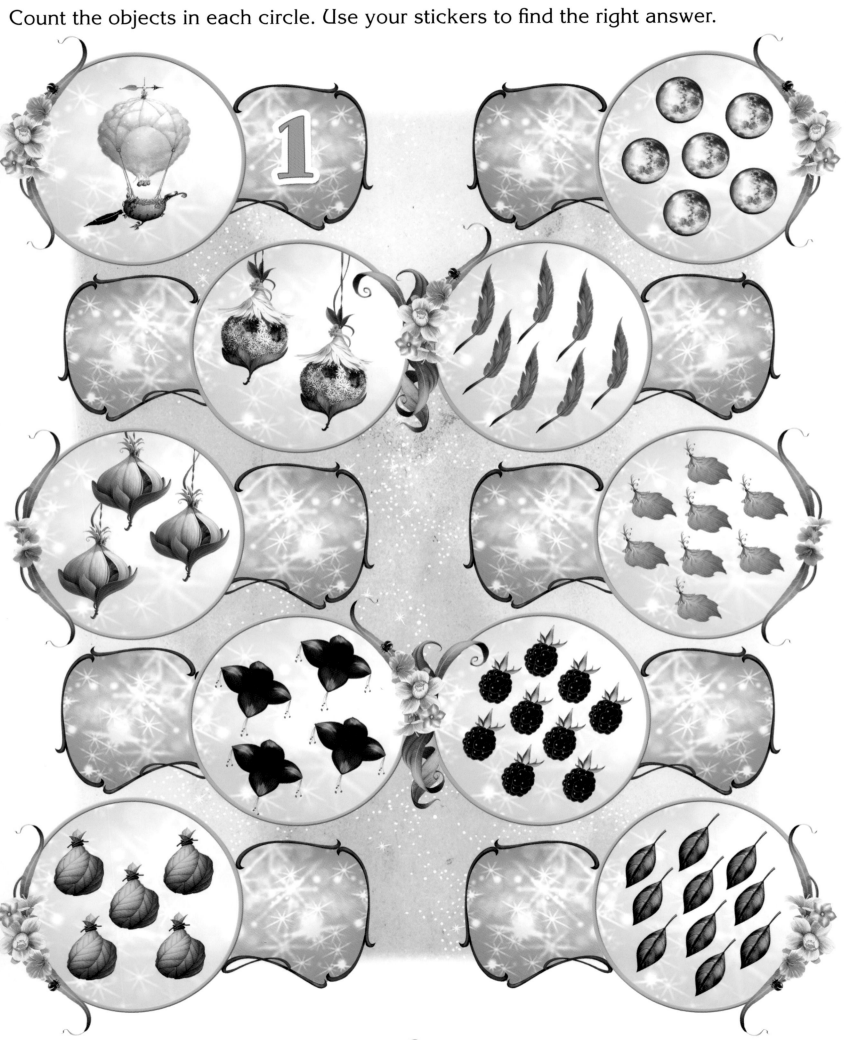

Time to Count

Help the fairies count each object from 1 to 10 using your stickers.

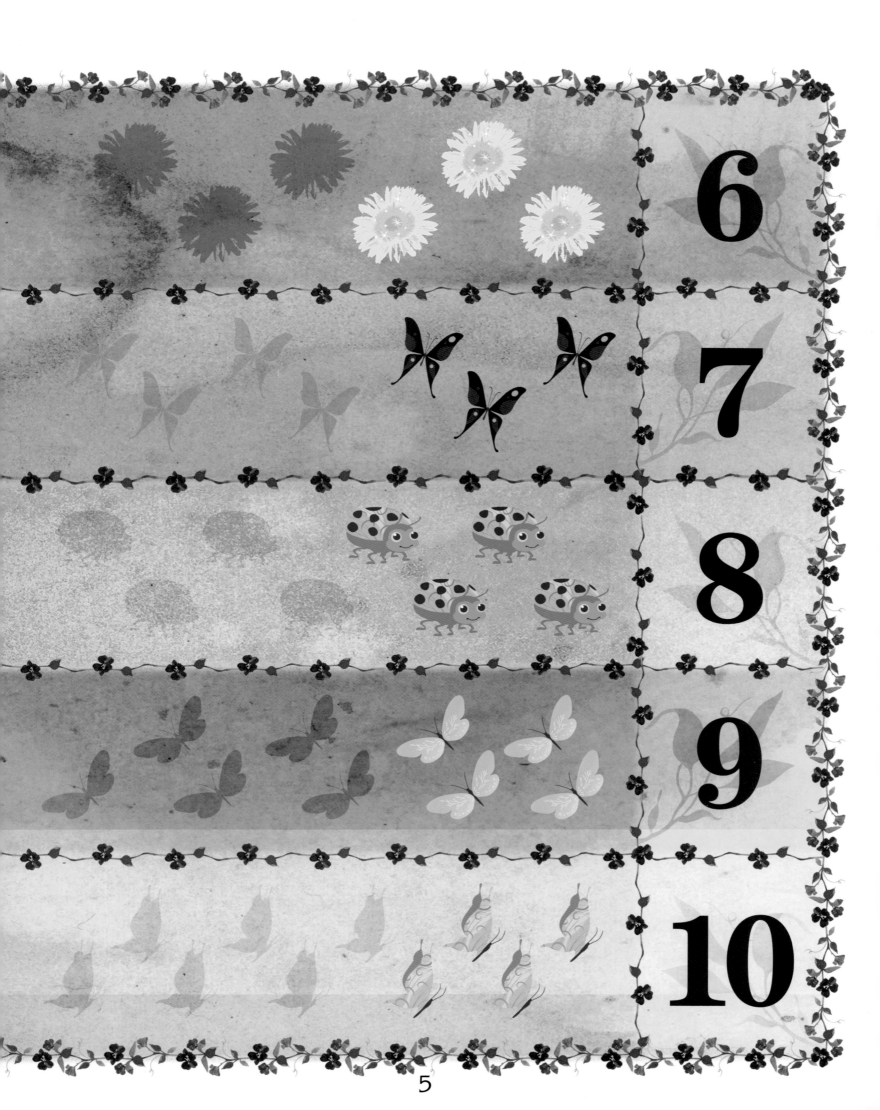

6

7

8

9

10

Pixie Hollow

The fairies are enjoying flying above Pixie Hollow. Decorate the scene below.

2 3 4 5 6 7 8 9 10

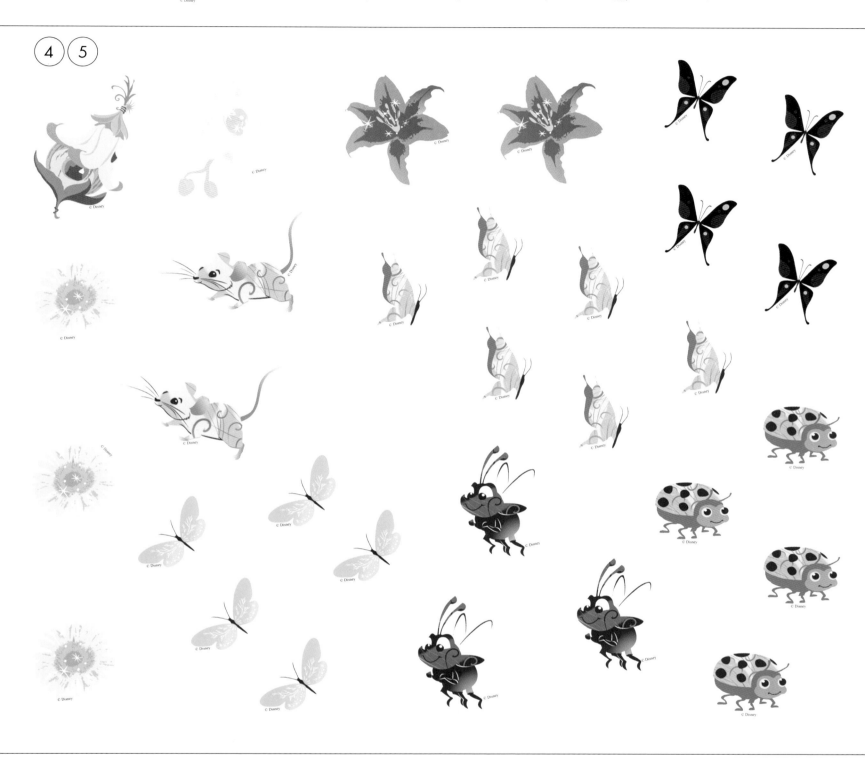

4   6   7

   1   4   2

Time to Add

Help Iridessa and Fawn solve the addition problems using your stickers.

2 + 2 =

+ =

1 + 5 =

+ =

3 + 4 =

Time to Subtract

Help Rosetta and Silvermist solve the subtraction problems using your stickers.

3 − 2 =

− =

7 − 3 =

− =

6 − 4 =

Springtime Square

Help count the objects in the scene by placing the correct sticker in each number box.

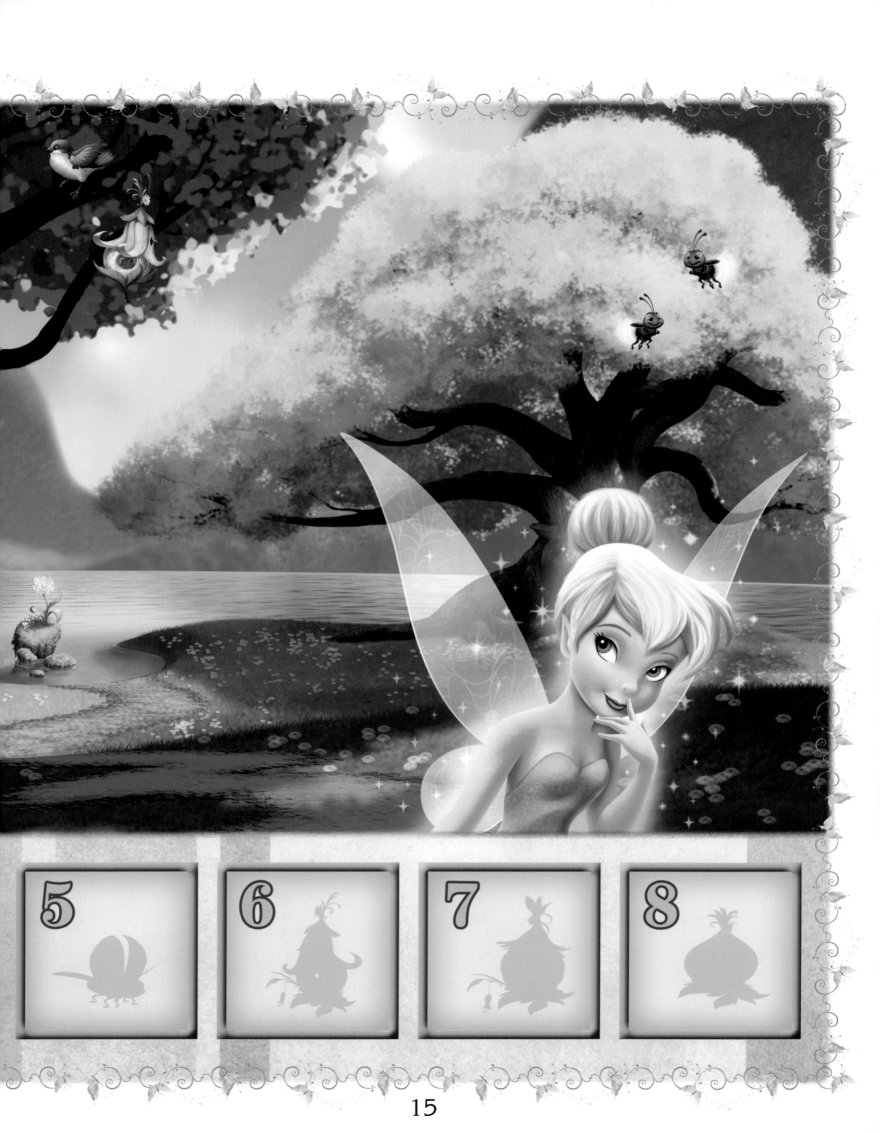

Fairy Equations

The fairies need your help to solve these equations using your stickers.

Colorful Fairies

Phidal

Color Match

These fairies are very colorful! Place each fairy in their matching color box below.

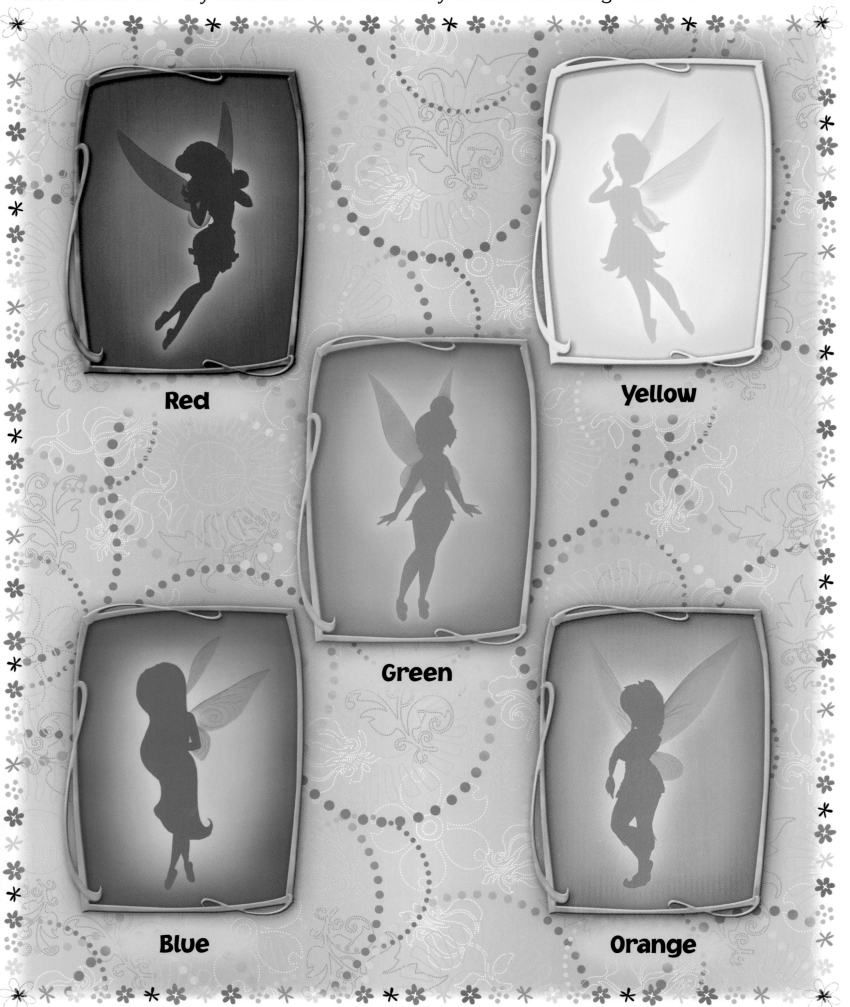

Red

Yellow

Green

Blue

Orange

Blooming Buds

Help Tink place each flower in its matching color box using your stickers.

Flying Friends

The fairies are having fun flying together over the water! Decorate the scene below.

Color Mix-up

When you combine colors you can create new ones. Help Rosetta mix the colors.

Blue + Yellow = Green

Yellow + Red = Orange

Red + Blue = Purple

Rainbow Colors

Help Iridessa match the color of each butterfly with the different colors of the rainbow.

Colorful Palette

Use your stickers to match each palette to the colors of what each fairy is wearing.

Gorgeous Garden

Rosetta needs your help to design a colorful garden using your stickers.

Fairy Quest

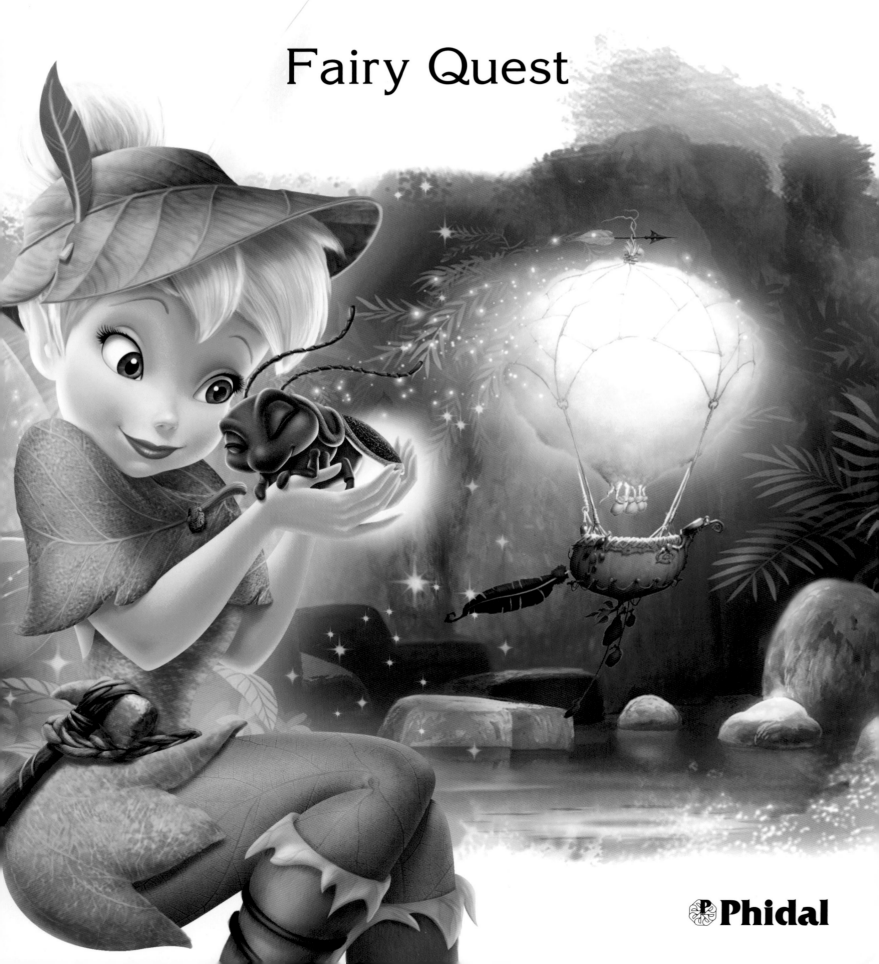

Phidal

Who am I?

Fairies love to play guessing games! Answer each riddle with the help of your stickers.

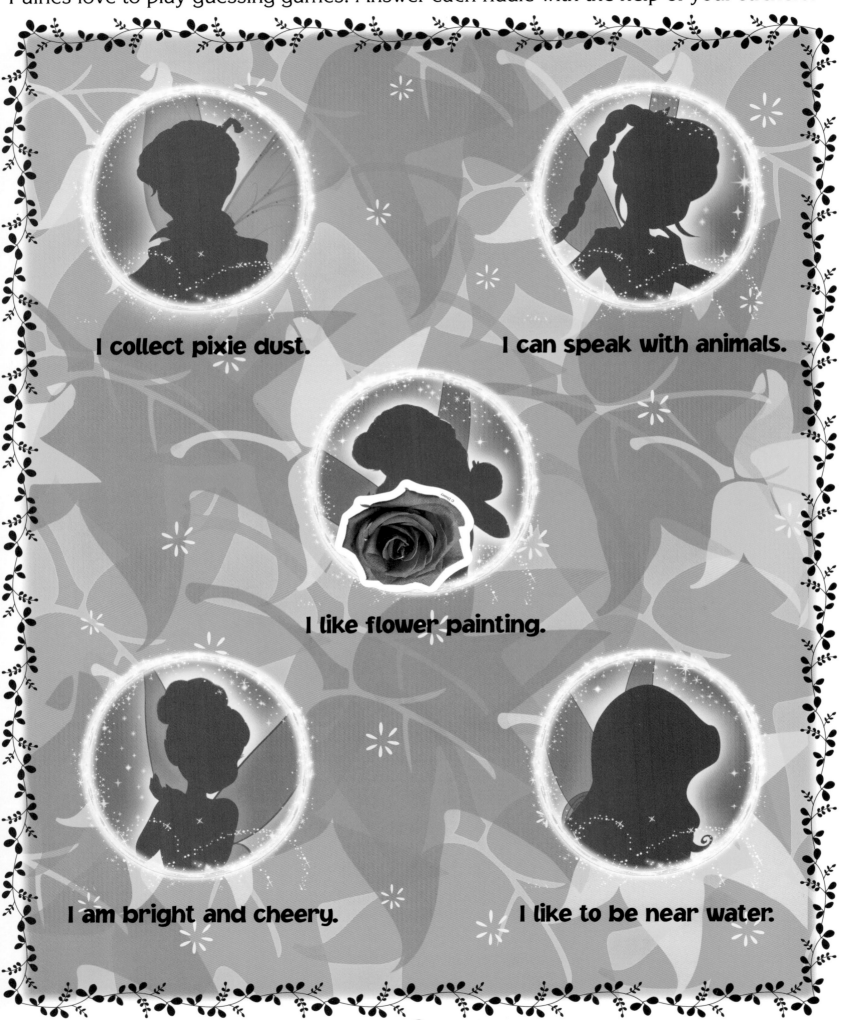

I collect pixie dust.

I can speak with animals.

I like flower painting.

I am bright and cheery.

I like to be near water.

Finding Opposites

Complete these fairy opposites by placing your stickers in the correct rectangles below.

Together   Apart

Sitting   Standing

Left   Right

Moving

Still

Angry

Happy

Front

Back

Babbling Brook

The fairies are enjoying their evening at the Babbling Brook. Decorate the scene.

Pixie Patterns

Use your stickers to complete these playful pixie patterns.

Tink's Quest

Tink needs your help to match each object with its name using your stickers.

Mirror of Incanta

Tink's House

Tink's Balloon

Autumn Scepter

Moonstone

13

Let's Count!

Use your stickers to help the fairies count how many things are in each portrait.

Pumpkin Patch

The pumpkins are ready to be picked! Recreate the scene below.

About the Author

CHRISTIANE JORY graduated from NYU's Tisch School of the Arts and, after thirteen years in New York, returned to her native Los Angeles. She is constantly exploring creative ways to survive for the starving artist. She first learned to cook during her year abroad in Paris; limited funds and market hours were the catalyst, which then lead to a job in a French vegetarian restaurant that didn't always pay its vendors. She had to quickly find ways to get through a night of hungry customers with bottom-of-the-barrel provisions. This experience plus her discovery of the food items available at 99¢ Only Stores led to the two years of nights and weekends it took to test and write *The 99¢ Only Stores Cookbook*. Jory is currently writing two new books, works for a DVD game production company, and resides in the Hollywood Hills with her rescued dogs, Minnie and The Pup.